D1212074

Nothing is too difficult if one has determined to do it.

(WHERE THERE'S A WILL, THERE'S A WAY. ALL THAT IS REQUIRED TO ACCOMPLISH ANYTHING IS DETERMINATION.)

世上无难事，只怕有心人。

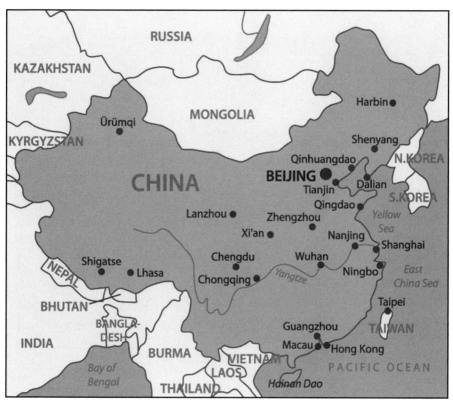

Map of China - pavalena/Shutterstock.com

© Can Stock Photo Inc. / marzolino - Old illustration of Beijing walls and gate. Created by Lancelot, published on Le Tour du Monde, Paris, 1864.

"Gary's book captured the soul and spirit of our joint venture journey!"

Yommei Yanagiba
CEO
Yingda International Leasing Co.
(a joint venture of GE and State Grid of China)
Beijing, China

"Anyone who understands the incredible opportunity ahead of us as the 'Asian century' unfolds will find this book of value. A global mindset in a hyper connected and turbo charged world is essential. This book brings together the foundations and tools you need to be part of an exciting future. Three authors all bring their unique experiences together creating a must read book for anyone who wants to be more effective, culturally aware and Asia capable. I just wish that this book was available when I started my 20 year long career living and working in Asia."

Hamish Tyrwhitt
CEO
Leighton Holdings
Sydney, Australia

"As a global CEO with operating companies in China and the U.S. I appreciate the value this book brings to global executives. Global mindset is an increasingly necessary skill for success in the 21st century."

Yoshiaki Fujimori
CEO
LIXIL
Tokyo, Japan

"Leaders at every level will welcome "Global Mindset Leadership" – a handbook and a great gift for leaders of the future."

Frances Hesselbein
Awarded Presidential Medal of Freedom
President and CEO, Frances Hesselbein Leadership Institute
New York City, New York, United States

"As an American I've had the good fortune of working outside the US for over 20 years for GE Capital and other multinational companies. My learnings gained during that time, more than just a few by hit or miss experiences, across many different European and Asian countries have significantly broadened my depth as a leader developing, and leveraging, a global mindset. Global Mindset Leadership would have saved me time as it provides a solid foundation for leaders looking to either better prepare themselves for global assignments outside a traditional Western business environment or to broaden and hone their existing base of multinational experience. Perhaps, most importantly, Global Mindset Leadership also provides an appreciation of the challenges many US-based companies face today in an ever increasing global economy. Gary, Donny and Marilyn's book outlines not only a strong foundation for working in today's global economy but also presents the reader with many tools for building their own personal leadership toolkit."

Jan Van Ekeren
CEO
Bank of Ayudhya
Bangkok, Thailand

"As China becomes more relevant in the rapidly changing global economy, leaders will need to understand new cultural values and behaviors to develop a truly Global Mindset. Global Mindset Leadership provides essential insight into how to grow as a leader to navigate business through this changing new world."

Ian Edwards
CEO, Managing Director
Leighton Asia, India & Offshore
Hong Kong, China

"Today, leadership development requires successful navigation across distinct cultures, legal environments and individual motivations. Global mindset is the new skill for the coming decade. This book provides important contextual insights into China & USA cultures as well as critical tools for emerging and senior business leaders."

Jay Gould
CEO
American Standard Brands
Piscataway Township, New Jersey, United States

"Gary has been working with GE in China for a while. He has developed a unique perspective of how western organisations can be successful in China. His latest book provides readers with a wonderful bridge between Western and Chinese business practices and breaks down the complex differences in an understandable way. A must read for business people wanting to navigate doing business in China."

Mark Hutchinson
CEO and President
GE China
Shanghai, China

"You add much value to your readers. The book will be a helpful resource to Chinese and American managers."

Mansour Javidan, Ph.D.
Director
Najafi Global Mindset Institute & Garvin Distinguished Professor
Thunderbird School of Global Management
Phoenix, Arizona, United States

"Multicultural competence is essential in most businesses today whether we are dealing with our peers, employees, clients or large organizations. The authors of Global Mindset Leadership have given timely and in-depth consideration to the complexities of Western and Chinese alliances, and show the way to working together for mutual benefit.

Beginning with historical antecedents and the current context of hitherto unknown speed of communication and fast-paced organizational change, they quickly move to the essence of multicultural competence which is the leader's capacity for self awareness and reflection. To develop multi-cultural competence we must diligently work at uncovering our own beliefs, attitudes and feelings regarding other cultures whilst simultaneously observing and responding effectively to the different cultural heritage of others. Global Mindset Leadership demonstrates the insight and openness which we all need if we are to overcome roadblocks and maximize the benefits of working successfully with Chinese and Western cultures."

Keryl Egan
Clinical Psychologist
Sydney, Australia

"Clear, insightful, and practical reference for any executives to do business with China. Gary's expertise and understanding of Asian culture helps establishing synergy between China and Western business practices. One of the best references for this subject."

Kenji Uenishi
COO
LIXIL Global Company
Singapore

"Although the title suggests that the book is specifically about navigating business cultures in China and the USA, the Global Mindset principles drawn herein are applicable to navigating any number of diverse business cultures to achieve set business objectives in any preferred business destination.

The book is the blueprint that simplifies the complex architecture of diverse business cultures seeking to identify and achieve common business objectives globally.

Juxtaposing business cultures of the two biggest global economies, allows the authors firstly to filter out principles and practices that would be detrimental to business relationships while at the same time distilling from this process, principles that enhance inter-cultural harmony.

Charles Moyo
Managing Principal
Lenong Marketing
Johannesburg, South Africa

\"With the benefit of hindsight and having endured establishing and operating a construction business in China, I certainly wish I'd met Gary years ago and had the benefit of the insight that Navigating China and US Business Cultures provides. I found myself nodding in agreement, mostly in regard to mistakes I made and misunderstanding of the culture I was working in. This book shortens that learning curve, from setting context around business relationships to expectations on outcome timelines. It bridges the gap on how we can get closer to achieving a global mindset in the Sino-US market place."

Boyd Merrett
CEO Leighton Offshore
Former Operations Manager Leighton China
Dubai U.A.E.

"Gary is unique in the coaching field and his insights are invaluable. His knowledge of cross-cultural styles and differences represent tools that no executive who deals in Asia should be without."

Gregg Feinstein
Managing Director and Head of M&A
Houlihan Lokey
New York City, New York, United States

"This book is invaluable because it captures in simple terms issues that are critical for success when working globally from the power houses of China and the US. Dr. Gary Ranker speaks from years of practical experience but his experience is different from most. His observations come from working intimately as a coach with executives challenged to successfully lead global organisations. He is with them to celebrate great achievements and also there through some of their darkest hours. Donny Huang, a leading cross-cultural management specialist draws on his thirty+ years of experience measuring cultural differences and running cultural awareness programs. He has assisted many organisations to understand differences constructively. Marilyn McLeod combines her skills as an author and her experience as the executive producer of the US TV show Consider the Possibilities to bring lateral thinking and creativity to applications of a global mindset.

The book describes many truths that while in plain view, are often invisible to us in the hurly burly of corporate life. When he talks about a global mindset, Ranker says to have a global mindset is to get beyond believing what has worked for us in our organisation in our country, will work to the same degree in another country. The words are his, the italics are mine. The phase to the same degree illustrates the point that working with a global mindset opens up enormous opportunity to leverage different approaches to great advantage, but to achieve the advantage you need mental agility to set aside assumptions and be open to, absorbent of, and then creative with, the many different ways people like to operate. For example success for business ventures in China is in part about having the right relationships, while success in the US requires knowledge of relevant laws and regulations. Combining the two opens opportunities "with the ultimate goal of blending the differences in business cultures and folding them into one another to ensure a strong result". McLeod's strengths in lateral thinking and creativity provide examples of how a global mindset provides new ways through old problems and opens opportunities made possible by the platform globally digital technology gives to us all.

Huang's contribution includes an elegant and engaging new 'intelligence'. To IQ and EQ he adds CQ. And CQ won't disappoint fans of a global mindset. It consists of three, inter-related, self-sustaining competencies. Increases in-depth self-knowledge, help develop more cross-cultural awareness which leads to the development of more extended values which impact self-knowledge.....This virtual circle sits comfortably with Confucian ethics and Western views of adult development. It is a profoundly satisfying model.

The book combines information, tools and stories that will be of interest to Chinese, Americans and others who are looking to overcome the self-limiting nature of the wonderful Frank Sinatra lyric 'I'll do it my way'.

Ann Whyte
Managing Director
WhyteCo Coaching, Change & OD Consulting Pty. Limited
Sydney, Australia

"This book primes us for a new understanding: The most potent currency of business today is a global mindset."

Wendy Johnson
President and CEO
Worldwide Association of Business Coaches
Sidney, British Columbia, Canada

"I've worked with Dr. Ranker for several years. He has a unique ability to take you out of your own world view, and help you understand how others perceive you. He challenges and motivates you to adapt to new environments in a positive and self-reinforcing way."

Stephen Ezekiel
Hong Kong, China

"Anyone preparing to do business in China should read this book first. Truly a must read for Human Resources and line managers alike."

Denise Sinuk
Director of Programming
Human Capital Conferences and Seminars
The Conference Board
New York City, New York, United State

"Don't be a bull in a China shop. Read Global Mindset Leadership: Navigating China and US Business Cultures! As an advisor to international entrepreneurial CEOs and a Globalization Skills Consultant - who has also spent 15 years living and working outside of the US - I dare to consider myself to be somewhat of a highly advanced student of global mindset leadership. However, without question, had I read Gary's book prior to embarking on past business initiatives involving organizations in China and Hong Kong or prior to working at CUNY as an occasional adjunct lecturer instructing Chinese students, I might have broken a little less of the precious porcelain. Of course to my benefit, Gary has navigated me away from breakables before, in his role as Emeritus Advisor to one of the Thunderbird, School of Global Management's largest alumni organizations, where I also serve as the President of the NYC Chapter.

Victoria Cox
New York City, New York, United States

"I've had the pleasure of knowing and working with Gary for a number of years. Observing Gary coaching senior executives is a fascinating process. Actually, it's more of a transformation. Week after week, month after month levels of self-awareness improve. Interactions become more strategic. Personal style becomes more situational. A more efficient and effective leader emerges.

Over the past few years Gary has devoted his unique experience and skill-set towards working with Chinese executives in Beijing and Shanghai, and helping leaders on both sides of the Pacific benefit from growing a "Global Mindset". This means becoming a better leader in an increasingly globalized world, and navigating the intricacies of Chinese and Western business and social cultures.

Gary provides an invaluable bridge between East and West, one which is underpinned by decades of experience working with CEOs and senior leaders of the world's most respected organisations."

Patrick Vizzone
Regional Head of Food & Agribusiness, Asia, Institutional Banking, National Australia Bank, and Independent Non-Executive Director, China Agri-Industries Holdings, COFCO Hong Kong, China

"The writing that articulates the importance of managing change before it manages you has been on the wall for some time: management sage Peter F Drucker predicting "an established company which in an age demanding innovation [creating new value] is not capable of innovation is doomed to decline and extinction."

The challenge for C-suiters is immense, given the Kiplingesque chasm of comprehension that lingers when doing business between East and West.

Dr. Gary Ranker's Global Mindset Leadership shatters plenty of shibboleths to discover a Deng Xiaoping-inspired "one venture, two approaches" path towards business prosperity. Beyond the myriad differences between Confucian-ethic-based norms-meets-Western rule of law, freedom and accountable government, there are, reassuringly, striking similarities, not least that both cultures value and appreciate constructive feedback, with victories celebrated.

As a business correspondent my job is to be skeptical, yet only a Luddite would dismiss the provocative, timely and trenchant insights Dr Ranker et al offer up. Even where I may disagree, I remember an important lesson of my experience: I am almost certainly going to be proved wrong."

Carson Scott
Anchor & Chief Business Correspondent
Sky News Australia
Sydney, Australia

"Marilyn and her co-authors have written an important new book which helps Americans and Chinese to better understand each other and forge closer business relationships. Our world is becoming more interdependent with every day. This book helps the reader develop their global mindset, a requisite for success in the 21st century."

Nathaniel Branden
Psychotherapist, Founder of Psychology of Self-Esteem, Former
Associate of Ayn Rand
Los Angeles, California, United States

"If Chinese culture has always baffled you, this book is the key to unlock its mysteries. If this book came earlier, it wouldn't take one year for my manager (American) and me (Chinese) to build the trust and know how to work together. This book not only shows the evolution of Chinese culture and society, but also helps you develop cultural competency, as well as provides very practical tips. I'm recommending this book to every leader who desires to have a global mindset, lead a global team and do global business successfully."

Qiu Zi
Leadership & OD Manager
Lenovo
Beijing, China

"Gary Ranker is a true global thought leader bridging the gap between the Western and Eastern world that we all live in today. He has created a unique way of communicating, advising and consulting at levels that truly touch the human spirit regardless of their culture. Yet he also finds ways of weaving in the obvious differences and nuances in the most artful way. This book is a magical view into the global world that we sometimes struggle to make sense of and understand. Gary and the co-authors help boil all of this down to clarity that will help guide leaders for many years to come"

Steve Rodgers
Former CEO
Homeservices of America, Berkshire Hathaway
Currently entrepreneur/owner Real Living Lifestyles Real Estate,
Berkshire Hathaway
San Diego, California, United States

"Over the past few years many books have been written about the importance of having a global mindset, but few if any have given you a roadmap to develop this critical leadership capability. Global Mindset Leadership fills this void and not only provides you with a roadmap to become a true global leader, but deep insights that will change the way you think."

J.P. Elliott
Vice President
Talent Management, The Brink's Company
Richmond, Virginia, United States

"China, the "emerging superpower", continues to go through structural reforms and the foremost objective is to maintain social harmony for a country with a diverse population of 1.3 billion. On the other hand, the US, the "developed superpower", has to embark on a path to "re-develop" itself to maintain its global competitiveness. Changes are in order for both. The need to accept each other as equal global partners and collaborate constructively will require a "global mindset" and "cultural competency" which are articulated very well in this book. How to navigate global cross-cultural relationships is always an art.

As Dr. Ranker puts it, "There is no universally correct way to do things". To get things done in a land of rapid development with change being the norm, it is worth remembering a famous saying of Chinese leader Deng Xiaoping, "Cross the river by feeling the stones" - a pragmatic approach, and one step at a time without a full process map as the situation is extremely dynamic and fluid. As a business leader traveling in the unknown waters, this book has practical and useful advice to help you navigate and stay on course."

Nancy Ku
Shanghai, China

"Gary is uniquely positioned to share his vast knowledge of globalization. While many claim to possess a global mindset, Gary's lives it, and here he shares a number of very help thoughts for business people to expand their global capability. This book provides a thoughtful reminder about the richness of culture and how subtle differences, if mastered, can create both opportunity of learning and effectiveness. Anyone from the most savvy global leader to those venturing across borders for the first time, will learn and benefit from this read."

Stephen Patscot
Spencer Stuart
Chicago, Illinois, United States

"Gary has been a thought leader in global leadership and diversity for decades. This new book provides refreshingly clear insights about how to adopt a global mindset in order to do business in the East. After having lived and worked in Beijing, I am certain that applying Gary's advice will lead to better results when conducting business in China. It is worth the investment of time to read."

Yolanda Lee Conyers
Vice President, HR Operations & Chief Diversity Officer
Lenovo
Beijing, China

"China is morphing into an 800 pound gorilla in economic and military spheres, and some feel that it may displace the aging 800 pound gorilla that the United States is. Perhaps or perhaps not. But there is no denying that China is certainly doing a lot of nudging. So it behooves every intelligent citizen, and certainly business persons, to understand why and how China is 'different'. Global Mindset Leadership does an excellent job of highlighting these differences in easy to understand language, as well as suggesting ways to work with such a different world view.

For example, Americans think in terms of permits as something to think about only when law requires. The Chinese have a mindset that permission is required for everything. In America we focus on rule of law and endeavor to encapsulate all kinds of contingencies in a legal agreement. Chinese are offended by this. They prefer trust in a relationship as it evolves over time.

Obviously there are many minefields that could blow up unexpectedly when there are such differences in how one approaches business collaboration. Reading this book makes that blowup less likely to happen."

Srikumar Rao
Author of Happiness at Work
New York City, New York, United States

"Gary is a rare individual who very early in his career eschewed a traditional career path, leaving the US to work for a German firm. In doing so, he learned some early lessons on the importance of a global mindset as an essential ingredient for effectiveness in business, and developed a passion for global business. He has since consulted with clients and helped develop the global mindset for executives around the world. During his career he has witnessed the rise of globalization and the successes and failures of Fortune 500 companies' attempts to become truly multinational companies.

Gary, Donny and Marilyn now turn their attention to China and U.S. business cultures, and how to instill a global mindset in both Chinese and U.S. business executives who must lead and manage diverse teams. For many companies the stakes have never been higher. The authors challenge the biases and preconceived notions common to both sides, and offer some surprising findings. The book provides practical suggestions on how to meld the very different cultures, respecting the differences and building on the inherent strengths of both."

David Hanson
Cisco Systems, Inc.
Shanghai, China

"All readers, no matter where they come from, whatever their political stands, will find much to stimulate their thinking in this book. It offers insightful views based on the authors' rich experience working with the top joint ventures in China. The most commendable feature of this book is the 'neutral perspective point' which many books lack. That's the key to the truth. The book answers for us 'What's the value in Chinese culture? What's different about the way the Chinese think? Why do many negotiations get stuck?' This book may make you feel a little bit uncomfortable at the beginning. It requires self-understanding and an open mind to learn new things. But as you read it through, you will find the objective and rational approach of the book has led you on the road of truly understanding cross-culture global management."

Wei Lu
Beijing, China

"In their important new book Global Mindset Leadership, Dr Gary Ranker, Donny Huang and Marilyn McLeod share key lessons for US firms seeking to improve their chances of success in China by asking us to move out of our corporate comfort zone – analytics – and into the challenging area of our implicit cultural assumptions and unconscious values. During my own 40 years as a strategic adviser in Asia I have learned – often painfully - that the financial, legal and analytical skills I built at business school were a valuable starting point – but that it has been the skills to understand complex social and political networks, and to build long term trusted relationships based on mutual respect which have made the difference between success and failure to our clients in the region.

The book's 'Global Mindset' concept, with it's stress on 'harmonious alignment' of Vision and Values, and of 'Know How' and 'Know Who' – is a useful construct to refocus attitudes and priorities. When combined with the book's portfolio of practical tools and processes the 'Global Mindset' offers a valuable supplement to traditional approaches to building a sustainable China business, where often, as the old saying goes, the contract may be the beginning of the negotiations."

Ian C Buchanan
Senior Executive Adviser to, and former Asia Pacific Regional Chairman
Booz & Company (formerly Booz Allen Hamilton)
Sydney, Australia

"Excellent insights into global cross cultural dimensions - this book is quite unique in its approach, providing a scholarly and broad study of doing business in culturally differentiated territory. It is impossible to sustainably succeed in business without being culturally relevant, and this book is a must have tool for those engaging in global business, especially on the US-China dynamic."

Jim Samuel
Academic & Managing Director
IAAI
New York City, New York, United States

"China has already made a major impact upon world business landscape. There is no doubt China's commercial presence will rapidly expand over the next decade. However, navigating the complex milieu of social interaction between the US and Chinese business cultures is proving to be quite a challenge for all. Many beneficial business ventures have come apart, simply because both sides did not properly adopt a global mindset. There are no others wiser than Ranker, Huang and McLeod in this area, who have considerable experience living and working on both sides of the Pacific. As the CEO of a company regularly doing business in China, I await its publication - and thank you for this gift of Global Mindset Leadership!"

Brian O. Underhill, Ph.D.
Founder & CEO, CoachSource, LLC
California, United States

"There is no more important market in today's global economy than China. Business leaders must understand how this market functions in terms of culture, history, values, leadership styles and mindset if they are to succeed here. In Global Mindset Leadership: Navigating China and U.S. Business Cultures the authors capture the critical nuances essential to successfully navigating and understanding China's complex, vibrant, and evolving business environment."

Terri Nissen
Sr. Director, Alumni Relations
Thunderbird School of Global Management
Phoenix, Arizona, United States

"Global Mindset may sound like a simple concept. In the old days, it would have been "manage China from New Jersey". Now, it would be "put an American expatriate in Shanghai for two years". These are fine, but to truly manage the cultural differences requires appreciation of deep-rooted Value. The trouble is that Value is not something written on the poster of the shop floor such as "Safety is our Value", or "We care for our employees". Values are not written nor spoken.

The two chapters on "Merging Business Culture" and "Joint Ventures" show deep insight into the topic of Global Mindset. Process versus People. Decision-making and Authority. These are all interesting and thoughtful topics. In the new world, the ability of managing a JV, or just in general, managing US business in China and (they are happening faster than you think) managing Chinese businesses in the US, will define an executive's career."

Albert Wong
Shanghai, China

"Leaders are on top of their roles when they act from their deepest values, instincts and capabilities. They tap into these fundamental qualities to solve problems most of the time with the right frame of mind. To further enhance a leader's competency is to possess and develop a global mindset with a natural curiosity about other cultures and the way businesses are conducted in order to achieve greater probability of success. This book Global Mindset Leadership is certainly a book to read for students, business leaders and anyone who is interested in understanding the business practices and cultures between China and United States. There is no better way to learn than to hear directly from the authors of this book who have extensive knowledge, practice and experience in this area."

Jimmy Wee Tek Tan
Singapore

"'Immeasurable curiosity' of the bottomless (never ending) challenge and 'blood-pumping tense feeling' to step into a new world are key, and the origin toward establishing a global business. Perhaps curiosity and tension are the basic components of a global mindset.

In reality in business, maintaining the critical balance between 'global integration' and 'local responsiveness' in order to operate in harmony is most important. Global integration provides a 'platform for practice', while 'local responsiveness' ensures successful execution of the practice.

It cannot be changed that people have the most important role to execute or perform the above global integration. Since a person is a person, the mindset that a person possesses determines how and why he/she will utilize potential and take action. Whether it is US or China, this important theory applies anywhere in the world.

Mr. Gary Ranker, who is my executive coach, goes on the journey with me in exploring true global leadership. In addition to his remarkable knowledge and experience, his faithfulness and sincerity have motivated the curiosity and tension within me, and have made my journeys fulfilling and worthwhile. Discovering your life time coach is a treasure for your life.

Toshimasa Iue
Former President & CEO, SANYO Electric Co., Ltd
Current EVP & CEO
LIXIL Global Company, LIXIL Corporation
Tokyo, Japan

"A lot of people & organizations have talked about the need for a 'global mindset' but it has never been laid out in such a clear & articulate manner before. It is an essential 21st century skill for success in today's ever-growing global environment. Gary, Donny. & Marilyn have helped define what a Global Mindset is, and showcase it as a more tangible & practically applicable skill. Getting this right is a critical step in transforming people, and through them, businesses, from being 'International' to 'truly global' in their approach. While China & the US are the primary examples in the book, they can easily be replaced by most relationship-oriented & task-oriented countries and contrasted in a similar manner. An outstanding & necessary read for those wanting to be truly global, which I believe will set the direction for many to follow."

Vikram Cardozo
Sr. HR Leader Asia Pacific GE
Kuala Lumpur, Malaysia

Global Mindset Leadership lays out a future picture by presenting compelling facts and strong reasons for each of us to develop our global mindset. The three authors bring a trifecta of experience that describes a world changing economically, politically, demographically, socially and culturally. These are structural changes that will affect us all. Global Mindset Leadership presents a way to learn, understand, and use these changes to our advantage."

Chris Coffey
Executive Leadership Coach
Marina del Rey, California and New York City, NY, United States

This book makes three major contributions to leadership and management. First, it provides a historical context for the cultural differences between China and The West. These cultural differences present opportunities and challenges for Western multi-national companies who are interested in or already doing business, in China and/or with Chinese Companies. Second, it describes these cultural differences through a structured framework. Finally, it defines and recommends an approach to meet the challenges and seize the opportunities resulting from the cultural differences. The solution is a "Global Mindset", a concept which will undoubtedly become as popular as "Emotional Intelligence" and "Positive Psychology".

Dharma Chandran
Chief HR and Corporate Services Officer
Leighton Holdings Limited, Sydney, Australia

Gary Ranker deeply understands people leadership, and the intricacies of leadership that are vital to success. He brings that depth of understanding and a real clarity to this significant issue - Global Mindset - which is so vital in today's world. Gary has been successful across multiple cultures and countries. He is outstanding at understanding the nuances of different corporate and national cultures. His command of the facts, his ability to simplify complex people issues, and his deep experience bring a sense of what is possible with the right approach and mindset.

Kerri Thompson
MD Bancassurance and Customer Experience
ANZ
Sydney, Australia

© Can Stock Photo Inc. / marzolino - Old illustration of Yamoun gate, Beijing. Created by Therond, published on Le Tour du Monde, Paris, 1864.

Global Mindset Leadership

Navigating China and U.S. Business Cultures

Dr. Gary Ranker
Donny Huang
Marilyn McLeod

Executive Excellence Publishing

Published by:
Executive Excellence Publishing
112 East 3800 North
Provo, UT 84606
801-607-1871

For information on other products and services by the Authors, contact:

Marilyn McLeod
760.644.2284
Marilyn@CoachMarilyn.com

Library of Congress Cataloging-in-Publication Data:

Ranker, Gary, 1942-
    Global mindset leadership: navigating China and U.S. business cultures / Gary Ranker, Donny Huang, Marilyn McLeod.
    ISBN: 978-1-930771-43-7
    1. China. I. Gary Ranker, 1942- II. Business. III. Title.

Printed in the United States of America.

If one doesn't plan for the future, he will soon have troubles in the near term.

人无远虑，必有近忧。

© Can Stock Photo Inc. / marzolino - Old illustration of Ma Tao, Chinese locality between Beijing and Tianjin. Created by Lancelot, published on Le Tour du Monde, Paris, 1864

Dedication

For Shan. Thank you for letting me see a different view of the world through your eyes. More than anything else this has deepened my understanding of global mindset.

— Dr. Gary Ranker

For my wife Tian. Thanks for her continuous support, encouragement and understanding. And for my grandmother, who taught me to dream and inspired me to learn and grow.

— Donny Huang

For Violet Panzram, my fourth grade teacher and friend later in our lives. Ms. Panzram first expanded my global mindset through her assignments: Writing letters to pen pals from distant lands, and to famous authors. My author choices were Dr. Albert Schweitzer and Herbert S. Zim. I still miss our conversations and adventures, and our walks through the woods.

— Marilyn McLeod

© Can Stock Photo Inc. / ryanking999 - Traditional Chinese painting of old tree with cloud and mist.

Contents

Chapter 1: Understanding Global Mindset   1

Chapter 2: Tracing History   15

Chapter 3: Confucian Ethics and Politics   43

Chapter 4: Generational Differences in Chinese Society   69

Chapter 5: Cultural Dimensions   83

Chapter 6: Context and Rules   105

Chapter 7: Developing Cultural Competence   117

Chapter 8: Merging Business Cultures   129

Chapter 9: Joint Ventures in China   161

Chapter 10: Global Mindset Applied   183

Resources:
Assessment Tools   193

References   204

About the Authors   207

© Can Stock Photo Inc. / ryanking999 - Traditional Chinese painting of high mountain landscape with cloud and mist.

Foreword

Foreword written by Marshall Goldsmith, *New York Times* best-selling author of *What Got You Here, Won't Get You There*, and ranked as one of the top ten Most Influential Business Thinkers in the World at the bi-annual, global Thinkers50 ceremony in London November 2013.

As an executive coach, teacher and speaker, I have the opportunity to travel around the world. So far, I have visited 89 countries and hope to make it to 100!

In my 37 year career, I have observed an incredible movement to increased globalization. In the past, most leadership was domestic. Leaders from their own country managed people from their own country and sold products made in their own country to people in their own country. Those days are gone. Today most leadership is global.

We are all becoming global citizens. The more that we can learn about other cultures, respect their ways of getting the job done and develop a global mindset, the more than we can maximize synergy and minimize unneeded mistakes.

I have great admiration for the work done by Gary Ranker. He is one of the world's most-respected executive coaches. I have had the privilege of knowing Gary since the late 1980s, when we worked together at GE in the early days of coaching. Over the years we have shared ideas and done our best to help each other. Gary has developed a deep focus on coaching senior leaders with international responsibilities

– most recently in China. He helps leaders develop the kind of global mindset that will facilitate their success as they work around the world.

I have known and worked with Marilyn McLeod for over ten years. We have worked together on many projects and collaborated on several articles, including "Peer Coaching" and "Thought Leadership: It Comes from the Outside and Inside" (published by Leadership Excellence). Marilyn has recently developed a mobile application of my work in conjunction with Thinkers50. She has now published twelve books and has established a wonderful working partnership with Gary.

Gary and Donny Huang have been colleagues for years and are both graduates from the top ranked, Thunderbird School of Global Management. They have collaborated on several projects with major organizations. Based in Beijing, Donny leads one of China's most respected cross cultural educational groups. He helps people from both the West and East become more culturally sensitive to each other.

Global Mindset Leadership: Navigating China and US Business Cultures is a book written by three very skilled professionals. It goes deeper than the surface level of cultural differences and talks about historical and generational factors that come into play when working in China. If you come from a Western culture, it will help you understand the Chinese ways of doing business and to see the world from their point of view. It can help you successfully navigate in your journey to build a global enterprise. It can also help you develop transferrable skills that go beyond China and apply to any international assignment.

I invite you to read this book and to apply what you learn. A wise person learns from experience. An even wiser person learns from someone else's experience!

China is becoming increasingly relevant to everyone in the West. It is becoming more relevant every day. Learning how to work across cultures will become one of the most important qualities for the leader of the future.

Having written or edited 35 books myself, I know when a book has value. Use the wisdom in this book to help you make a difference in China and around the world.

Marshall Goldsmith
Rancho Santa Fe, California
January 2, 2014

© Can Stock Photo Inc. / saransk Red dragon.

© Can Stock Photo Inc. / patriomonio -
Dragon fighting silhouette.

Preface

We define ***global mindset*** as the willingness and ability to step outside one's own base culture, and to respectfully understand there is no universally correct way to do things.

From that perspective, some interesting observations can be made. Certainly there are great differences between Chinese and U.S. cultures. There are also many similarities. Surprisingly, going beyond surface appearances, we find that some things which seem to make us different, are actually quite similar. And some things which seem similar on the surface may have very different connotations within each culture.

For instance, both cultures have within their traditions the concept of a dragon. To the Westerner, a dragon conjures up images of a fearful creature that needs to be conquered. By contrast, Chinese embrace the dragon as a benevolent creature that symbolizes strength, wisdom, good luck and power.

We invite you, within the pages of this book, to set aside any preconceived notions of either the U.S. or Chinese culture, and learn from our exploration of each other's ways. From the vantage point of the other culture, you may even learn some new things about your own.

The payoff of having a ***global mindset*** is greater awareness that will help you navigate more effectively through business interactions and strategies on your way to a successful initiative with the other culture.

© Can Stock Photo Inc. / marzolino - Old view of Hong-Kong. Created by Sabatier after watercolour of Trevise, published on Le Tour du Monde, Paris, 1860

Acknowledgements

We wish to thank Lu Wei, Beijing and New York City for his help with illustrations and Chinese proverbs, and the many people who helped us review the manuscript. Especially we wish to thank those people who provided us with interviews: Cat Midkiff, David Hanson, Joan Emrich, J.P. Elliott, Julie Qiu, Karen Zong, Nancy Ku, Patrick Vizzone, Victor Lu Wei, Yommei Yanagiba and the many other people who generously gave us their comments. Thank you to Ken Shelton of Executive Excellence Publishing for his editorial advisement. Illustrations courtesy of Can Stock Photo and Shutterstock. Cover images of dragons: ©Can Stock Photo Inc. /Digitalstudio and /marish.

© Can Stock Photo Inc. / nicholashan - Chinese ink painting.

Great heroes see things in the same way.

(GREAT MINDS THINK ALIKE.)

英雄所见略同。

© Can Stock Photo Inc. / ryanking999 - Traditional Chinese painting of high mountain land-scape with cloud and mist.

Understanding Global Mindset

Gary Ranker defines ***global mindset*** as the ability to step outside one's base culture, and to understand there is no universally correct way to do things. He asks his clients to realize that persons in other parts of the world have different beliefs than they do, and different ways of doing things that work for them. To be effective as a global leader, we need to take this into consideration when we do business with others.

Developing a ***global mindset*** means accepting that our values and our ways of doing business don't have the same meaning, or perhaps even work, for our counterparts in other cultures. To have a ***global mindset*** is to get beyond the trap of believing that what has worked for us and our organization in our country, will work to the same degree in another country. It may or may not. But it won't work to start with the assumption that we will be successful forcing our ways onto the other culture.

Looking at Global Mindset

How do most of us make decisions? By default! We choose brands, styles, food, hobbies, friends, co-workers and careers that feel comfortable and familiar to us. We are often shaped by outside factors that push and pull us in different directions. Some people say it takes 10,000 hours to truly master a skill. How many of us plug away at the uncomfortable edge of the learning curve for those 10,000 hours just to learn a new skill? Most of us prefer to pull back and enjoy the experience of short-term gratification, albeit at some lower level of expertise, rather than continue pushing through those many unrewarding hours to real mastery. Mastery has become a lost art. Even more difficult is the task of understanding a trade or a skill outside of the context in which we learned the skill. When we are asked to remove ourselves from our common practices and rituals, and shift to a mindset that is conscious of global influences and impressions, most of us may feel some hesitancy and caution.

Consider the basic act of communicating. Let's assume for a second English is your first language. In the United States, Canada, and many other parts of the world, you would have no problem communicating with a taxi driver, hotel clerk, or restaurant owner. As long as he or she spoke English, you will be fine. But if you found yourself in a foreign country, one whose natives speak little English, the simple task of asking for directions or paying for a bottle of water could be enormously more complicated.

It's not easy to immerse oneself into an unfamiliar culture for an extended period of time. This is not a common practice and we often feel somewhat shy and not as confident in our abilities. It's even more difficult to go to a distant land with the goal of establishing or building a successful business in that new culture. If we can't communicate on a personal level, how can we do so on a corporate level? Speaking the language is just the first step. Once we can overcome the language barrier, the next step is to study the culture and behavioral norms. There seems to be a never-ending learning curve—ranging from local business laws and practices, managing talent, how business decisions are made, how to appeal to the local consumer, to how people think and relate to one another. In the global marketplace talent and consumers come from multiple geographic locations, making the cultural environment so multifaceted it's hard to imagine anyone responding with finesse to every cultural equation. It takes time, effort, and the willingness to immerse oneself into the nuances and experiences of a whole new world.

Cultures differ as much as creatures in the ocean. There are thousands of regions, cultures, business practices, and socially accepted behaviors. To understand the context of your global scenario is to have a fast track to achieving your overall business goals. Simply because one formula works in one global market doesn't mean it will work in another. But as an individual who has decided to read this book, you already recognize this notion. In the past twenty years, China has rocketed into the spectrum of global importance and business development. Some of the biggest business deals and agreements are occurring in this remarkable part of the world. While the speed in which business is accomplished in China is extraordinary, it comes with an entirely new set of business norms and behavior.

Conditions change rapidly in China, so assumptions and agreements must remain fluid in order to endure. With each change in Chinese management and government, the all-important context changes as well. Relationships must be revisited and adjustments made to fit new political and cultural contexts for every new leader.

Why Care About Global Mindset?

If you're a middle level executive in the U.S. you might say, "My revenue right now is not dependent on global sales, so why should I care?" The truth is, power has shifted in the world and we're all encouraged to recognize the need for a *global mindset*. We can't continue to use old models. Hanging onto old models could spell failure.

As Chinese move more toward *global mindset*, Chinese traditions of respect for authority will begin to blend with the Western sense of entitlement and their tradition of questioning authority. Chinese value a sense of patience and oral contracts, and Western cultures value deadlines and depend on legal documents signed before any work begins. A Chinese organization's Chairman explained to Gary, "I don't understand the Western way of thinking. With all of these rules, where to park or not, how to use a toothbrush in the right way, labels on cords that warn against dropping the appliance into the bathtub, how people are to be treated ... it looks to me like a society of leaders who don't trust their population."

An investment banker in New York City told us, "The Chinese don't understand how to play our game. They tell us they want to acquire a company. We tell them the rules of how to get involved in mergers and acquisitions, but then they don't play by our rules. They don't understand that U.S. companies may not be able to do the deal without getting the necessary paperwork signed by the deadline, and many deals fall apart as a result. This is a disappointment to both sides, because both sides were really ready to make the deal." As more power shifts to China, our rules may gradually become less effective, and we'll have more success as Western executives by finding ways to work more effectively with the Eastern way of doing things.

The profitable, marginal opportunities are more costly because they're more sophisticated, but they're more available because people haven't gotten to them yet. Opportunities within existing markets can become the new revenue producing centers. Young professionals and new wealth bring new demand for luxury and trending products. For instance, Starbucks and iPhones have become staples in Chinese professional circles. Luxury eyeglass manufacturers have realized their frame design didn't allow proper placement for where the Chinese eye is located, so new designs have been created for China. Red has replaced other product colors bound for the Chinese market. Another trend showing up in some industries is similarity in product design across cultures. Ford is moving toward only a few basic models globally which they'll customize to the local market.

The United States is not the only country being drawn from an insular experience into the larger global arena. China is taking advantage of the opportunity to become proficient in working with a wider variety of cultures regarding their products and services, and how people want to be managed. There will be emerging entrepreneurs who rival larger corporations for market share. Even large conglomerates will have to grow and adapt.

As a company whose products involved interaction between people, Hallmark was ahead of its time as they began to think of their base as a 'social expression business'. They would look into their local market to determine the unique characteristics of this market. They would develop unique products within their core line of greeting cards, party goods, candles, and gifts that reflected a keen sensitivity to the local culture.

Other corporations who produced products that more easily crossed international cultures could simply set up a sales office in a new country, and the people who wanted that product just needed to be informed they were there. So much of early U.S. success was simply creating awareness of the product, consumer benefits and how to use it. For instance, the company would advertise disposal tissues instead of handkerchiefs that needed to be washed, and blenders were shown to make work in the kitchen much easier. Innovations coming from the United States were welcomed and sales were good.

Over the years Gary has noticed that many U.S. leaders, even those with international responsibility, are very U.S.-centric. It's been possible as Americans for us to think of ourselves as having the right answers, that we have the highest evolution of systems and ours is, of course, the best way. Europeans have become more accustomed to the fact there are other ways of doing things. They've grown up in close proximity to a variety of other cultures, and cultural awareness is just part of their reality.

Historically in the United States we've been allowed, and even encouraged, to be quite insular. It's not on our radar to really regard others within their own context. Rather than valuing and understanding the other culture, we've often merely seen them as an opportunity to expand distribution of our products and services. Because of the forcefulness of our nature we've been successful selling concepts and products to the world, however it's not always been with sensitivity to the local culture.

Because in recent history we have been the dominant culture of the world, people in other cultures did buy our products and services. This lulled us into an attitude that we did have the best. We could say, "There's the evidence, people are buying our products and services, we must have the right

6

answers." The reality was helped by the fact that we were the only game in town, and we were more forceful.

When Gary chose to study and then work outside the States, he recognized the United States had what could be considered an economic empire. Whereas the British empire involved military might, the U.S. held economic might. In business school Gary was trained to help manage our economic empire. The U.S. had better marketing techniques and better systems for running companies. These, among other things, helped us to be successful worldwide.

The world is going through a transition now. The U.S. continued to evolve during the past 50 years into organizations that are quite different from traditional Western structures. There has been an evolution from hierarchical to matrixed organizations, and now beyond the matrixed organization. This allows for more democratic ideas, and for empowering people in the West to make effective decisions. In the past era as large corporations were heavily involved in selling their concepts and products all around the world, companies began to develop an international operation. The next evolution will underscore the need for *global mindset*, because we are not alone in the world. Other organizations have emerged and are different, and are successful in their own context. To the extent that we want to be successful in other countries, it doesn't work to go into the situation with an ethnocentric frame of mind. We need *global mindset*.

How does one even begin to approach this environment successfully? We suggest it begins with a mind open to learning, and slow to criticism and judgment of what may be unfamiliar to us. This would include sincere interest and perhaps even enthusiasm for the unknown. We are confident this book will help you develop greater awareness to help you ride the waves of new cultural experiences.

> # A fool does not ask.
> # The one who asks is no fool.
>
> ## (IF YOU REALLY WANT TO LEARN, YOU HAVE TO BE HUMBLE ENOUGH TO ASK QUESTIONS AND REVEAL YOUR IGNORANCE.)
>
> # 愚者不问，问者不愚。 -Confucius

Putting it into Context

Within China there are different business cultures. Leadership styles and employee expectations for behavior and workflow vary between multinational companies, local private companies, and government owned organizations. State Owned Enterprise (SOE) organizations are the most traditional. Local Chinese companies still follow traditional customs, but may also incorporate Western concepts into their business systems. This is especially true if they are led by the emerging breed of young Chinese entrepreneurs. Multinational companies operating in China bring their Western cultures, and Chinese employees working within the multinational company learn how to operate within this sub-culture. Leaders in a multinational company may come from several base cultures. They learn to work in ways that show both understanding of and respect for local Chinese employees.

Consider Huawei, the privately held major telecom equipment manufacturer, Huawei is one of the most global companies in China today. The founder is said to combine both Chinese and Western wisdom. The top leaders work like a Chinese family—all of them are very close, and they trust each other. To incorporate Western wisdom, a Western multinational company helped streamline their product development and management systems and to organize the company to work more like a Western company. Since top management is like a hierarchical Chinese family, the decision-making process is very nimble and not transparent to those outside the management team. When a decision is made, execution happens very systematically as employees are trained to respect authority and follow directives from their superiors. A combination of East and West business practices has enabled Huawei to grow into a large global company, acting in many ways as a bridge for the connectedness between Eastern and Western business practices.

The capacity for a *global mindset* is particularly important when two very different cultures need to coordinate. A specific Chinese example from this experience is a joint venture (JV) between a Chinese SOE and a U.S. multinational company. The SOE is run very differently from the multinational organization. Think of this from the JV CEO's perspective. Although the CEO might have come originally from the U.S. company, or from the Chinese side, as CEO they are expected to be neutral. In one specific successful example, the CEO oversees a JV which has a 50/50 percent split where neither organization is dominant. The U.S. company is a very successful iconic company. The Chinese SOE has almost two million employees, and is very tied in with the government in China. Both companies are very proud of their success. And the two companies are almost diametrically opposed to one another in terms of management systems, values, process and decision-making—in almost every way.

In this example the CEO has worked diligently to weave a careful path between these two enterprises. The CEO spends each day focused on expertly balancing all the facets of a new venture. The CEO must express sensitivity to both cultures, while moving things forward. Both companies have a different decision making process, and each is learning how to work with the other. The CEO must have an ability to maintain sensitivity and neutrality as a leader. The CEO is required to look with value at each side of the JV while working outside of their own base culture as an individual. The valuable experience that the CEO has gained inside of their base nationality, and their base corporate culture, must be retained, taught and blended with skill. All of this is done while absorbing, respecting and adapting to the new corporate and national culture.

Global Mindset in China and the U.S.

Having a *global mindset* means different things to Americans and Chinese. From a U.S. point of view, having a *global mindset* indicates a natural curiosity about other cultures, the ability to get outside our base culture, and to see the world through someone else's eyes. From a Chinese point of view, having *global mindset* might mean following Chinese customs and culture while incorporating Western concepts into their business systems, practices, and processes. It becomes less an action of putting on someone else's glasses, and more actually blending other shades of color with ones own.

Chinese and U.S. children grow up with different values. What is characteristic of a good Chinese child? The Chinese traditional culture values obedience. What is characteristic of a good American child? U.S. Americans value independence and creative thought. These early expectations carry into

10

adulthood, into the culture, and finally are brought with them into the workplace.

The Western practice of brainstorming sessions brings to light some key differences in practice between the two cultures. Westerners expect people to think out of the box on their own, and to participate in brainstorming sessions. These expectations will often fall flat in a Chinese context until there is mutual trust among participants. Building this trust takes time. Acquiring this trust might require having lunch with individuals, getting to know them personally and showing interest in their families.

U.S. employees would understand their U.S. leader s' expectation of brainstorming, so they offer ideas, thinking they are participating in creating synergy. They have a sense of many people contributing, and out of the many, they create something new. Chinese may be uncomfortable when pushed to get involved. In fact, they might just sit quietly on the sidelines. If U.S. leaders want the Chinese viewpoint, patiently working to develop this trust and synergy over time is important.

Chinese people are not trained to question authority or discuss ideas. They may feel vulnerable when asked to make comments that may criticize current policies or authorities. They may also feel uncomfortable verbalizing ideas that are not fully formed. Chinese value the act of taking time for personal reflection to find clear solutions. If U.S. leaders recognize this and take steps to help their Chinese employees engage in discussion, they will be more likely to gain more Chinese participation. This means building trust individually before asking anyone to share in public. While Americans often jump at the chance to shout their contributions loudly across a meeting room, Chinese people won't share their true feelings or what they think in any public, group environment where they feel unsafe. The Chinese perspective of a brainstorming session is that "You have a brain, but no storm." They prefer to study and weigh the information and come to their own conclusions.

After discussing this and coming to conclusions within the safety of private settings, the group experience can then be a harmonious expression of the consensus that was developed on a personal and private basis.

Chinese leaders working with U.S. employees might perceive public questions as impertinence, a challenge to authority, or even insubordination. Although within the Chinese context such verbal outbursts seem offensive, if the Chinese leader can look more deeply they might benefit from the concepts offered by outspoken employees. Companies worldwide send their employees to learn from U.S. companies that have changed the world with their ideas. Creative thinkers thrive on sharing ideas. If they feel their ideas are unwelcome, they may begin to look for employment elsewhere.

Freedom and democracy are strong Western values. Eastern people traveling West can learn to adapt their style to be more participative, and as a leader invite more participation in their decision making process. Communication and transparency are important in terms of building trust and working with Western cultures. From either a Chinese or U.S. perspective, *global mindset* involves being open to an entirely new paradigm without bringing in judgments and preconceived concepts from our own base culture.

As you journey through the following concepts and ideas, we invite you to consider reshaping your views and opinions of exactly how to operate from both a personal and business perspective. If you were to attempt to do business in China in the same manner you do business in the U.S., you would find yourself frustrated and unsuccessful. If you make the effort to understand the other culture, it will be easier to navigate through that culture more successfully. To do this, be open to new and different thought processes and management methods that work within the other culture, even if at first they don't seem to make sense.

**There is no mighty river
that isn't formed**

by many little brooks.

(GIANT OAKS FROM TINY ACORNS GROW.)

不积小流无以成江河。

13

© Can Stock Photo Inc. / Morphart - Great Wall of China, during the 1890s, vintage engraving. Old engraved illustration of the Great Wall of China.

Tracing History

In 2006 Harvard professor Niall Ferguson and the Free University of Berlin professor Moritz Schularick coined the term "Chimerica". In 2009, American economist C. Fred Bergsten initiated a name of "G2" referring to the group of the United States and China, to demonstrate the importance of U.S.-China relationship in the 21st century.

Xi Jinping, then Vice President of China, visited the United Sates in February 2012. He proposed "a new type of relationship between major countries in the 21st century" (*Xinxing Daguo Guanxi*) seeking to further solidify Sino-U.S. ties. President Xi mentioned that such a relationship would be characterized by "mutual understanding and strategic trust," "respecting each other's 'core interests'", "mutually beneficial cooperation", and "enhancing cooperation and coordination in international affairs and on global issues". Obama administration responded positively to this new initiative. Tom Donilon, Obama's national security adviser, summarized the administration's general reaction at some length in his speech titled *"The United States and the Asia-Pacific in 2013"* on March 11, 2013 in New York.

> *"I disagree with the premise put forward by some historians and theorists that a rising power and an established power are somehow destined for conflict. There is nothing preordained about such an outcome. It is not a law of physics, but a series of choices by leaders that lead to great power confrontation. Others have called for containment. We reject that, too. A better outcome is possible. But it falls to both sides—the United States and China—to build a new model of relations between an existing power and an emerging one. Xi Jinping and President Obama have both endorsed this goal.*

The "New Type of Relationship between Major Countries" most likely will dictate the future direction of Sino-U.S. relations. Besides announcing the new mode of relationship with the U.S., President Xi Jinping also proposed creating the "New Silk Road" Economic Belt. He described his vision to revive the ancient trade passage among central Asian countries and China when he addressed Nazarbayev University in Kazakhstan during his trip to G20 Submit in September 2013. A month later he restated the same goal in October 2013, during his trip to the 21st leaders' meeting of the Asia-Pacific Economic Cooperation (APEC) in Brunei. Xi called for rebuilding "The Maritime Silk Road" in his speech to the Indonesian parliament, aimed at enhancing the maritime partnership with 10 members of the Association of Southeast Asian Nations (ASEAN). There is some potential conflict in Obama's "Pivot to Asia" policy, which focuses on doubling the effort to build diplomatic, economic, people-to-people and security ties with the Asia-Pacific region in the 21st century, and to increase U.S. presence in Asia.

Sino-U.S. bilateral trade volume increased from only 1 billion U.S. dollars three decades ago to more than 500 billion U.S. dollars in 2012. The United States owes China over 1.3 trillion dollars in debt. Almost all U.S. large corporations have a presence in China. Recently the Chinese food company Shuan Hui acquired Smithfield, the largest American pork processor. AMC, the largest U.S. movie theater operator, was also acquired by a Chinese company. Economic activities will increase rapidly in the future, as the two countries are increasingly interconnected and interdependent.

Even though "Chimerica" and "G2" are probably the most important relationships in today's world, the two countries are vastly different in many aspects. China's two "Silk Road" policies, along with Obama's "Pivot to Asia" strategy, require China and the U.S. to interact quite a bit more than in the past, due to overlapping core interests from both parties in the region. In reality, when an established power is dealing with an emerging power, sometimes conflicts and disputes are inevitable. Generally speaking, the Chinese know more about America, than the Americans know about China. China has a long history and very different economical, political and cultural structure and system.

Historically, the U.S. and China relationship has dated back before American independence. It was Chinese tea, from Amoy (today Xiamen in Fujian Province), that the patriots had dumped into sea in Boston harbor that famous night in December 17th, 1773. Before American independence, there were already many Chinese goods and products in North America colonies, ranging from Chinese art, craft, Chinaware, to Chinese tea, etc. After the independence, the Americans

17

wasted no time going to China seeking trading opportunities. In these first years of American involvement in China, the new American government played a minimal role. Mostly the interaction involved trade and missionaries. In the 1830s, the first group of brave American missionaries reached Canton (Guangzhou today). They risked their lives, since the Chinese promised death by strangulation to anyone who got caught propagating Christianity. The initial governmental attempt to establish relations with China on a treaty basis started in the 1830s, during the administration of Andrew Jackson. Jackson sought to expand American trade in the Orient. He sent Edmund Robert on a mission to find new commercial opportunities in the Orient. Edmund Robert reached Canton in November 1832, but failed to establish any contact with local authorities. At the time, China was a powerful empire which owned about 30% of the world's wealth (see Chart 1). In July 3, 1844, the first treaty between China and the United Sates was signed. From

With sufficient effort, an iron rod can be ground into a needle.

(ALMOST ANYTHING CAN BE ACHIEVED IF YOU PUT ENOUGH EFFORT INTO IT.)

只要功夫深，铁杵磨成针。

the 1830s to the 1940s the Americans continued engagement of both political and business relationships with China.

The Silk Road

Chinese government has recently rejuvenated two ancient "Silk Road" concepts for its foreign policies to expand its interest in Central Asia and Southeast Asia. As mentioned above, the United States has intensive interest as well. The **Silk Road**, or **Silk Route**, is a series of trade and cultural transmission routes that were central to cultural interaction through regions of the Asian continent connecting the West and East by linking traders, merchants, pilgrims, monks, soldiers, nomads and urban dwellers from China to the Mediterranean Sea during various periods of time in history. (definition from Wikipedia).

The Silk Road extended around 4,000 miles (6,437 kilometers). It gets its name from silk trading, which began during the Han Dynasty (206BC – 220AD). The German terms "Seidenstraße" and "Seidenstraßen", 'the Silk Road(s)' or 'Silk Route(s)', were coined by Ferdinand von Richthofen, who made seven expeditions to China from 1868 to 1872.

The Central Asian sections of the trade routes were expanded around 114BC by the Han dynasty, largely through the missions and explorations of Zhang Qian (张骞), who was an envoy sent by the emperor. He became a Chinese national hero in history because of his effort in terms of developing partnerships with countries in the West. Chinese emperors protected the routes by extending the Great Wall and placed soldiers along the way to ensure the safety of the trade route.

Trade on the Silk Road was a significant factor in the development of Chinese civilizations, the Indian subcontinent, Persia, Europe and Arabia. It opened long-distance, political and economic interactions between the civilizations. Though silk was certainly the major trade item from China, many other goods were traded, including various technologies, religions and philosophies, as well as the bubonic plague (the "Black Death"), also traveled along the Silk Routes. In addition to economic trade, the Silk Road served as a way for cultural trade between the networking civilizations.

The main traders in the beginning were the Indian and Bactrian traders. From the 5th to the 8th century the Sogdian traders were dominant. Afterwards the Arab and Persian traders controlled.

A new railway spanning 11,179 kilometers (6,946 miles) from the bustling mega city of Chongqing, southwest China to all the way to Buisbury, Germany, is called a revival of the ancient silk road. The railway goes through Xinjiang, Kazakhstan, Russia, Belarus, Poland and Germany. The rail network was inaugurated in 2011. It is a joint venture between track operator D.B. Schenker, the Chongqing Holding Group, and the state railways of China, Kazakhstan and Russia. U.S. computer giant Hewlett Packard claims to have shipped more than 4 million notebook computers to Europe by train during this period. This replacement of the ancient silk road will expedite economic, cultural and political interactions among countries in the region, and serves China well in his quest to upgrade its economy.

The Maritime Silk Road

The Maritime Silk Road, like its overland counterpart, had its origins during the Han Dynasty (202 BC-220AD). The maritime routes opened by Emperor Han Wudi (who reigned 140-87 BC) provided access to the Roman Empire via India, marking the first oceanic route as well as the earliest marine trading route in the world. This enabled China to actively trade with overseas markets and establish foreign trade relations, and laid the foundation for the development of the Maritime Silk Road. The Han Shu Record (also known as *The History of the Han Dynasty*) kept the first complete vivid record on China's boats sailing into the Indian Ocean from the South Sea via the Malacca Strait in Southeast Asian waters. Han ships with silk would leave from Xuwen in the South of China's Guangdong Province, or Hepu in South China's Guangxi Zhuang Autonomous Region, and via the South Sea, would arrive in India and Sri Lanka—a transfer station, where pearls, colored glazes, and other exotic things could be bought back to China. Chinese silk was transported to Rome hereafter. Such was the early marine Silk Road.

In his book *Nature History*, Gaius Plinius Secundus, a knowledgeable scientist in ancient Rome, recorded, "four sailors from (today's Sri Lanka) left for Rome (during the Caesar Era). According to one of the sailors named Rutgers, both Rome and Sri Lanka had direct trade relations with China."

In his book *Secundus* describes the Roman Emperor sending envoys to China, presenting various such gifts as ivory and hawksbill turtles to the imperial royal court, which marked the earliest friendly relations between China and European countries. A direct route from the East to the West was therefore established.

During the Tang Dynasty (618-907 AD) Chinese ships would sail from Guangzhou across the South China Sea, thus pioneering the most important routes of the maritime Silk Road. In addition to transporting silk, the South China Sea routes stimulated both material and cultural exchange. Countries throughout Southeast Asia, South Asia, West Asia, and even Europe dispatched emissaries to China via the new maritime routes to establish diplomatic relations, purchase silk, and to engage in trade of all sorts. Silk, as the principal maritime trade commodity, flowed in a steady stream from China to other countries.

Profits from the maritime trade were one of the Chinese government's major sources of revenue during this time. The Tang, Song (960-1279), and Yuan (1279-1368) Dynasties all appointed special Commissions of Maritime Affairs at coastal cities including Canton (Guangzhou), Mingzhou (Ningbo), and Quanzhou. These offices were responsible for overseeing maritime trade and providing logistic support to foreign merchants in China. The maritime Silk Road thus became a conduit for promoting friendly relations and linking East and Europe.

Decades before Christopher Columbus sailed the ocean in search of a water route to Asia, the Chinese were exploring the Indian Ocean and Western Pacific and this solidified Chinese control over much of Asia in the 15th century. From 1405 to 1433, Admiral Zheng He in Ting Dynasty (1369-1466AD) commanded expeditionary voyages to Southeast Asia, South Asia, the Middle East and East Africa.

In the 21th century one of great drivers of global change is coming from the rise of China. Chinese tourists, now the largest source of potential international tourism, along with Chinese products, culture, technology, business people, students, and capital are reaching every corner of the globe through new Silk Roads.

22

Historical Economic Power Shifts in the World Economy

Year Country	1750	1800	1830	1900	1962	1980	1994	2004	2008	2010	2012
CHINA	32.8	33.3	29.8	6.2	2.8	2.4	2.1	4.7	7.4	9.4	11.5
USA	0.1	0.8	2.4	23.6	42.4	26.4	26.4	28.3	23.2	22.8	21.9
FRANCE	4.0	4.2	5.2	6.8	5.5	6.5	5.3	4.9	4.6	4.0	3.6
GERMANY	2.9	3.5	3.5	13.2	6.7	8.0	8.1	6.6	5.9	5.2	4.7
BRITAIN	1.9	4.3	9.5	18.5	6	5.3	4	5.2	4.3	3.6	4.3
JAPAN	3.8	3.5	2.8	2.4	4.5	10.4	18.2	11.2	7.9	8.6	8.3

Notes about the data:
From 1750 to 1900: Percentage of world total production.
From 1962 to 2012: Percentage of total world GDP

Sources: The Rise and Fall of the Great Powers, Paul Kennedy, *World Bank's annual World Development Report IMF Reports*

For Americans to understand more about China, it is necessary to put down their American cultural lens. There is an often-quoted story about what different people experience when touching an elephant. In the "Six Blind Men Touching an Elephant" story, when a blind man touching elephant's leg, shouting that elephant is like a tree trunk, another blind man touching elephant's stomach, arguing the elephant is like wall. Each one feels a different part, but only one part. In the same way, each new awareness of Chinese ways gives us one more helpful puzzle piece gradually describing the whole picture.

In order to understand China, we need to look at China historically and holistically. In 221BC, King Qing Shihuan, who first built the Great Wall and Terra Cotta Soldiers, united China, created the first Chinese united kingdom. This kingdom already had modern State's elements, mentioned by Professor Francis Fukuyama in his book *The Origins of Political Order: From Prehuman Times to The French Revolution*. Professor Fukuyama argues that the first modern State, which emerged in China in 3BC, 1800 years earlier than that in Europe. From the period of 221BC to 1911AD China experienced more than 10 centrally-controlled authoritarian dynasties. Even though the emperor changed in every dynasty, the political, economic and cultural system remained relatively the same throughout this period. This degree of continuity is extremely unusual in the world history. Chinese professor Jin Guantao called the unchanged social structure in Chinese history as "The Ultra Stable Structure".

In this structure family is the vital element. The large families formed the kinship social structure, which constantly maintained stability in the countryside level of Chinese history, serving as an important part of governmental body in every kingdom. The economic system was also built upon the family-based agricultural economy. Family (家) and State (国) are two undividable parts of The Ultra Stable Structure. The glue that connects the Family and the State is commonly accepted as Confucian ethics. Confucian ethics regulates Chinese society, and has created social order throughout Chinese history. The Chinese word for nation is 国家, which is a combination of Family (家) and State (国) .

The stable structure maintained its place of importance until 1840 when China was confronted and challenged by Western Civilization. This was demonstrated by the outbreak of Opium War. China's old social structure could not keep up with the development of the new industrialized world, which had been regulated by a new Treaty System with the birth of Nation States. Since then, with the decreasing of power, China has faced the invasion of Western forces, and has been learning how to adjust itself and how to adapt to the industrialized era.

October 1, 1949 was the founding of the People's Republic of China. At this time the government successfully fended off Western influence in the Chinese mainland. Initially China and the U.S. discussed establishing a formal diplomatic relationship. However, with disagreement from the Truman administration and the outbreak of the Korean War in 1950, China was forced to become an ally of Russia. With initial help from Russia China rebuilt itself from the debris of the World War II. China copied much from Russia, from architectural building design, governmental structure and educational system to the economic structure. From 1950 to 1972 there was little official dialogue between the two countries until February 1972 when Nixon visited China. On January 1st, 1979 China and the United States established an official diplomatic relationship.

Also in 1979 Chinese senior leader Deng Xiaoping initiated the Chinese social reform which introduced Western capital market principles. This began a reorganization of the means of production in China, transitioning from the rigid Russian style of a planned economic system. This helped China's competitiveness in the world economy, and made it

(Pay) one cent, (you get) one cent quality of the goods.

(YOU GET WHAT YOU PAY FOR.)

一分钱，一分货。

Cheap things are never good.
Good things are never cheap.

便宜没好货，好货不便宜。

The expensive aren't really expensive; the cheap aren't really cheap.

(EXPENSIVE THINGS ARE A BETTER BARGAIN IN THE END BECAUSE THEY LAST LONGER)

贵的不贵，贱的不贱。

possible for China's manufacturing capability to become very integrated into the world's supply chain over the next three decades. The United States embraced China's reform, and was one the first group of Western countries to invest in China.

However, even today, China is still in the process of transition from a traditionally Confucian-ethic-based society to a modern society, characterized by Western values such as rule of law, individual freedom, and accountable government. We believe that China is heading toward the future along a different path which will integrate Chinese Confucian ethics along with the Western values, creating a new sort of hybrid system that combines the best of the East and the West.

From this prospective it will be easier for people to understand that historically China has always been a centrally controlled State. Government has always been a vital part of Chinese society. For Western multinationals it is important to understand the government's role in business in China because the relationship between relevant government agencies and businesses in China is key to success.

As a growing major world manufacturer with a goal of exporting to other countries, China has evaluated foreign companies and initiatives in terms of:

- What percent of manufacturing is done in China.
- What management and governance expertise is brought to China.
- How many Chinese people are trained.

U.S. companies often want inexpensive labor and access to the Chinese market. Above all they desire profit for their shareholders. U.S. governing principles are rules based, and draw from 1,000 years of British law. Governing principles in China are context based and draw from the culture at large,

27

which has developed from extended family and 2,000 years of Confucian philosophy. Essentially, Chinese business is part of the extended family, and the central government is the head of the larger Chinese extended family. Though there are local laws on the books, the laws are intentionally written with sufficient vagueness to allow for interpretation as conditions change. China is learning more and more each day how to blend rule of law with their traditional systems.

In the U.S. personal relationships are also very important in business social interaction. Often times we hear the term: "It is not what you know, but who you know." This means that personal relationships also play a vital part in personal success in the U.S. In the U.S. friends are not expected to bend the rules for you. In China your friends expect you to go the extra mile for them, which may involve bending some rules. Building good relationships with the Chinese government begins with developing personal friendships with government officials and their associates. Success in any relationship involves understanding what the other party holds dear, and finding ways to help them get what they care about. Though there are vast differences in what people and governments value between China and the U.S., it is possible to navigate the differences more successfully with some understanding of their motivations and needs. In order to understand those motivations and needs, we need to explore larger topics that give birth to the two different social systems and governments.

The ideological differences between China and the U.S. have deep historical and cultural roots. The origins of American's current democracy date back to a culture in ancient Athens that believed in one man, one vote and individual rights. The structure of the American Rule of Law and system, along with the Constitution, can trace back to the Roman Republic. Ancient Greek philosophers Plato and Aristotle argued that

28

the great thing about adulthood is that an adult could be fully rational and had the ability to reason. All these elements from democracy, such as individual freedom, rule of law and rational reasoning are the basis of modern Western societies and governments. All of these elements are considered natural to most Americans.

On the other hand, the modern Chinese authoritarian structure dates back to as early as 221BC, China's first united kingdom. Qing built the Terra Cotta Soldiers, which are still on display today in Xian. Throughout Chinese history, Chinese social structure and government were very much built on the thoughts laid down by Confucius (551-479BC). Confucius believed that the collective good is always superior to individual interest. He emphasized filial piety which creates family order and responsibility with natural hierarchies. This form of organization has been replicated in society at large. Therefore, being aware of these different histories and roots will help Americans understand the reasons Chinese citizens behave as they do. Such things as respect for seniors and being obedient to authorities come natural to the Chinese. Terms such as democracy, citizen and science only began to be heard in China during the late nineteenth and early twentieth centuries. The concepts of individuals and rational reasoning are still very foreign in China. As a result, what comes natural to the Chinese may look very odd to the Americans, and vice versa.

On July 1, 2013 China passed a law called "Protection of the Rights and Interests of the People's Republic of Elderly People". The Constitution of the People's Republic of China stipulates that "Chinese citizens have the right to material assistance from the state and society when old, sick or unable to work", "Citizens above the age of 18 are obliged to support their parents" and "There must be no mistreatment of senior citizens, women or children". The basic laws of China, including the

Law of the People's Republic of China on the Protection of the Rights and Interests of Elderly People, General Principles of the Civil Law of the People's Republic of China, Law of Succession of the People's Republic of China, Marriage Law of the People's Republic of China, Criminal Law of the People's Republic of China, and Law of the People's Republic of China on Public Security Administration Punishments, all clarify the rights of senior citizens and stipulate the legal punishments for acts infringing upon their rights.

The laws provide that when living family members are separated from their elderly family members, they should visit them often. If a child doesn't visit their elderly family members on a regular basis, this is considered illegal. The law states that the relevant individuals shall be given administrative punishment. Their lack of attention to their elderly relatives will constitute a crime and shall be prosecuted as a criminal act. The law has been nicknamed "The Law of Go Home Often to Have a Look". On December 20, 2013 the first case was brought regarding this law. The court ruled in favor of a father in Beijing, who demanded that his two daughters take care of him. The 81 year old father, Yin Jinxi, complained to the court that his two daughters had not taken good care of him for the previous nineteen years. The court issued a verdict demanding that Mr. Yin's two daughters pay 1000RMB per month, and visit their father once every month. In addition, the story was published in the media, in a sense further punishing the daughters through public loss of face.

One wrong step can cause regret forever.

一失足成千古恨。

In a democratic society Americans develop a set of values that regulate their behaviors. The following is a group of values that Americans live by, according to American Anthropologist L. Robert Kohls.

1. Personal Control over the Environment

People can/should control nature, their own environment and destiny. Future is not left to fate.

Result: Energetic, goal-oriented society.

2. Change/Mobility

Change is seen as positive, good, meaning progress, improvement, and growth.

Result: Transient society geographically, economically, and socially.

3. Time and Its Control

Time is valuable-achievement of goals depends on productive use of time.

Result: Efficiency and progress often at expense of interpersonal relationships.

4. Equality/Egalitarianism

People have equal opportunities; people are important as individuals, for who they are, not from which family they come.

Result: Little deference shown or status acknowledged.

5. Individualism, Independence, and Privacy

People are seen as separate individuals (not group members) with individual needs. People need time to be alone and to be themselves.

Result: Americans seen as self-centered and sometimes isolated and lonely.

6. Self-Help

Americans take pride in own accomplishments, not in name.

Result: Respect is given for achievements, not accident of birth.

7. Competition and Free Enterprise

Americans believe competition brings out best in people and free enterprise produces most progress and success.

Result: Less emphasis on cooperation than competition.

8. Future Orientation/Optimism

Americans believe that, regardless of past or present, the future will be better, happier.

Result: Less value on past; constant looking ahead to tomorrow.

9. Action and Work Orientation

Americans believe that work is morally right; that it is immoral to waste time.

Result: More emphasis on "doing" rather than "being;" Pragmatic, no-nonsense attitude toward life.

10. Informality

Americans believe that formality is "un-American" and a show of arrogance and superiority.

Result: Casual, egalitarian attitude between people and in their relationships.

11. Directness, Openness, Honesty

One can only trust people who "look you in the eye," and "tell it like it is." Truth is function of reality, not circumstance.

Result: People tend to tell the "truth" and not worry about saving the other person's "face" or "honor".

12. Practicality/Efficiency

Practicality is usually most important consideration when decisions are to be made.

Result: Less emphasis on the subjective, aesthetic, emotional or on consensual decisions.

13. Materialism/Acquisitiveness

Material goods are seen as the just rewards of hard work-evidence of "God's favor".

Result: Americans are seen as caring more for things than people or relationships.

*Adapted from: *The Values Americans Live By*, by L. Robert Kohls

> **Give a man a fish, then he will have meals for a day; teach a man to fish, then he will have a skill to earn his living.**
>
> 授人以<u>鱼</u>三餐之需，
> 授人以渔终身之用。

Global Mindset Evolution

The evolution of *global mindset* has occurred at an exponential level. It started slowly, with North American and European companies familiarizing themselves with other parts of the world. Today it is common practice for even smaller local companies to enter into global opportunities. Those who embrace *global mindset* in their business practices find new ways to move forward into emerging opportunities, while companies unwilling to move beyond their old ways of doing things may find their future opportunities fading.

Our journey toward *global mindset* has spanned generations. The difference in the current global environments in both the U.S. and China can be studied through the evolution of the two cultures. They both rely heavily on personal development, corporate growth, dedicated leadership and

35

meticulous training to build the foundation for business growth. As each of these economies has evolved and matured, so has the general climate of the community. To more fully understand *global mindset*, consider how these fundamental concepts have evolved:

Personal Evolution. In many parts of the U.S. people are surrounded by cultural diversity. Interacting with people from other cultures is just part of the environment. In China most people are from the same ethnic group, so interacting with people from another cultural dynamic is unique. Gary grew up in the U.S. with a sensitivity to people from other cultures, always trying to learn as much as possible. This orientation has been key to choices he made during his career. He has been willing to put himself into unfamiliar and sometimes uncomfortable circumstances in order to experience or interact with people from another culture. As global ventures become more prevalent, more people find themselves in these multicultural circumstances. Gary suggests a sincere interest and receptive mind to cultural differences are valuable tools to navigate this new territory. This strategy will serve much better than trying to fit what we experience of new cultures into the limited categories offered by our own base culture of origin.

Corporate Evolution. Many years ago, U.S. globalization began with large American corporations which were successful selling their brand when they began to sell their products abroad. They were considered the trailblazers who paved the path for global opportunities. After a few years they set up offices in other countries. Usually they populated those offices with people from their offices in the U.S. Sometimes leadership was given to domestic leaders with little international experience. It was often a disaster. Some operations were not as profitable or successful because the leader had little affinity for the difference in culture. This is an example of the opposite of *global mindset*. U.S. corporations were often rewarding senior executives at the end of their career by letting them have some fun during those last couple of years. In other words, international operations weren't necessarily taken seriously.

But the evolution continued. Companies then started to develop manufacturing in other countries, and to set up an international division as part of their corporate organizational structure. Skip forward to today. Just as, from a personal standpoint, the ability to look through the eyes of someone from another culture and to get beyond cultural norms are a foundational part of *global mindset*, in the same way, the company operating globally will no longer have only the eyes or view of their country of origin. Instead they will be able to think of themselves as a globally oriented company that happens to work in various countries, and although they originated in the U.K. or in the U.S., they now have become something that's global. They begin to use talent and resources in different ways.

Leadership Evolution. In the beginning of the modern leadership movement, command and control was the prevalent leadership style in the West. Businesses operated using a very hierarchical leadership style where bosses were expected to know the answers, and people who reported to the bosses were supposed to be quiet and do what they were told. When Gary started managing he was told very distinctly by some of his bosses, "What you're doing, Gary, in terms of inviting participation in decisions, is up to you, but realize your neck is on the line. You don't have to be involved with people because most of us aren't. You are the boss. Just tell people what to do."

From their perspective Gary was acting in a revolutionary way for the time. Over the past several decades there has been an evolution in the West towards more participation by more people in decisions that affect individuals. There has been less

37

hierarchy, and a move towards more matrixed organizations. This evolution has been more prevalent in the West. *Global mindset* helps us realize that management trends we believe are correct in the West may not be correct in other countries such as in Asia. In Asia very often a strong leader and hierarchical organization are the desired norm.

In the West there has been an evolution of *global mindset* from having many expatriates over time. Now many organizations are looking for talent across the globe, taking a person from one country and putting them in another country so they are effectively growing *global mindset* talent. One example is a highly skilled third country national leader Gary works with in GE. He is originally from India, working for a U.S. company, and living in Tokyo. He speaks all the different languages one would expect. He is an example of someone who's a third country national being used in a very respected way by a multinational company.

Coaching Evolution. General Electric approached Gary in 1989 to be a change agent to support Jack Welch's vision for GE. The type of role Gary played at GE later became known as an executive coach. Originally Gary was asked to meet with executives and measure how closely their management style and objectives matched the organizational design outlined by Jack Welch. Gary would visit the executive onsite, interview them as well as their management team, and would then send a report back with results. Over the years this has evolved into a process now popularly called 360 degree assessments. Gary continues to interview his client's stakeholders in person, traveling to their location on a bimonthly basis, with weekly teleconferencing between visits. Gary's reporting with GE and other clients now tracks stakeholder comments and ranking on coaching themes. In addition Gary still tracks how well the executive exemplifies the company's leadership qualities.

As Gary works with global CEOs, the importance of clear and conscious behaviors that match the character of various cultures is increasingly a vital tool of cross-cultural effectiveness.

With a fundamental understanding of the evolution of the Western and Eastern cultures, we can begin to effectively evaluate the prism through which we view **global mindset**. If we choose to make a change in perspective, it helps to approach it with a receptive attitude. In life so much of what we can see is based on the glasses we look through. We all assess and interpret life's experiences in different manners. The prism through which we view our lives shapes the way in which we comprehend what we see, and then make choices that shape our behavior. In a global setting it is essential we acknowledge that different cultures will relate to very specific traditions and norms. These have been embedded in their minds through the manner in which they live their lives. It helps if we can simply accept this and become sincerely curious and respectful about the differences.

One can never finish learning.

学无止境。 **- Confucius**

The common thread in all of this is the ability to get outside of one's own skin, and to be able to look through someone else's eyes, whether as an individual or as a leader. The evolution of the *global mindset* is integral to the development of the global marketplace. It not only shapes it, it creates it. As you navigate the remainder of this book, keep these concepts in the forefront of your mind, as they will offer you valuable context to understand where we came from so you can appreciate where we are.

This chapter has painted a picture of the business practices in China. But history is just one integral piece of the overall puzzle. While it remains the foundation for what has followed, China is recognized as a culture driven not just by its history, but also its political and ethical make-up. In the next chapter we will explore the relationship between China's history, politics, and ethical beliefs.

**Eloquence is not as important
as quality execution.**

(ACTIONS SPEAK LOUDER THAN WORDS.)

说得好不如做得好。

© Can Stock Photo Inc. / ryanking999 - Traditional Chinese painting.

Confucian Ethics and Politics

With Chinese history in mind, let's take some time to consider the Confucian ethics and politics that drive much of the Chinese business practices. These practices have spanned generations and are embedded into the fundamental teachings for even the youngest Chinese children. They transcend individuals to corporations and are an integral part of the everyday beliefs and behaviors of the Chinese. In China there is a direct relationship between business, politics and philosophy. Even today the educated Chinese businessmen are often called Ru Shang (儒商), which literally means "Confucian Businessmen". Understanding the interplay of these factors within the Chinese culture illuminates aspects of doing business in China.

Confucian Ethics

Confucian ethics are different from anything in North America. China is among a very few countries in the world that builds its culture or orthodox school of thought on the philosophy of ethics, moral standards and some useful principles. Many countries in the West build their culture around religion. Confucius was a philosopher, not a religious figure. These practices are completely foreign and to understand the underlying principles, we have to evaluate the relationship the Chinese have with these important ethics that transcend all of the Chinese culture.

Historically Chinese children grow up immersed in the classics, and base much of their way of life both personally and professionally on what they've learned from the classics. Today, even though government has lowered the importance of teaching these principles and values, Chinese society is still very much regulated by Confucian ethics. The following is a brief overview for the benefit of U.S. based executives who did not have this background in philosophy. Confucius emphasized personal and governmental morality, correctness of social relationships, justice, and sincerity. Respect for elders and family extends to the ideal model for government. Moral character is also an important focus.

"Do not do to others what you do not want done to yourself" was an earlier version from Confucius of the Golden Rule, which is known to those of us who grew up in the U.S. Reciprocity is highly regarded, which includes being careful that one imposes on others only positive conditions one would want for oneself. Children strive to understand and follow examples of morality given by Confucius, including developing skilled judgment as opposed to knowledge of rules, or rules of behavior. Logical, reasoned argument and ethical ideals are not as highly valued as in the West. Methods are conveyed more indirectly, nonverbally, or through innuendo. Context becomes very important in order to understand how to apply these concepts. Students of Confucius reflect on how to respond according to Confucian ideals, and how to improve so their response grows in greater alignment with those ideals. Interpretation favors a duty to family and friends before duty to community. Someone following Confucian ethics would choose different strategies in different situations and contexts.

Sincerity and developing knowledge create a balance with one another. Virtuous action is an important concept. Knowledge leads to sincere thought and virtuous action. It is said that a virtuous disposition without knowledge can be susceptible to corruption, and virtuous action without sincerity is not the true ideal. On a personal level knowledge and sincerity are also important. Someone highly evolved would love learning for the sake of learning, and simply would value righteousness for the sake of righteousness.

Confucian ethics is described through personal value traits, which include 仁 (Benevolence),义(yi), 礼 (rituals), 智 (Wisdom), 信 (Integrity), 恕 (Tolerance), (Loyalty) and 孝 (Filial Piety). Those traits are integral to relationships and interaction with others. Expectations and standards are defined for five relationships:

1) A ruler to their subject
2) A father to his son
3) An elder brother to his younger brother
4) A husband to his wife
5) Between friends

Rén 仁 (Benevolence) represents five basic virtues: seriousness, generosity, sincerity, diligence and kindness. Rén is the virtue of perfectly carrying out a person's responsibilities towards others. This may include benevolence, humanity, being authoritative or selfless. Rather than applying rules from a divine source, Confucius' moral system focuses more upon understanding others and empathy. To develop a spontaneous rén response (guiding intuitive action) was considered better than following rules of yì. Confucius said that virtue finds a balance between extremes. For example, a person who is properly generous gives the right amount—not too much and not too little.

Lǐ 礼 (rituals) is based on three important concepts of life within Chinese culture: 1) ceremonies, which can include sacrifice to ancestors and deities, 2) political and social institutions, and 3) etiquette in terms of personal behavior.

Confucius relied upon quality leaders to develop lǐ through their actions to build an ideal society. Doing the proper thing at the proper time, keeping a balance between maintaining existing norms to perpetuate an ethical social fabric, and violating them in order to accomplish ethical good, are qualities of lǐ. Training cultivates a person's ethical judgment about when lǐ must be adapted in light of situational contexts.

Yì 义 The concept of Yì is difficult to convey in English. It may be thought of as doing the right thing for the right reason. When you receive favor or help from others, it is the practice of paying it back. Self-interest is also a factor. It is not necessarily a problem to pursue ones own self-interest, but one practicing Yì would be looking for ways to enhance the greater good as opposed to fulfilling one's own self interests.

A Confucian ethic became the orthodox school of thought in the Han Dynasty (202 BC-220AD). With the disintegration of Han, Confucianism lost its prominence and gave way to Buddhism and Taoism, dominating intellectual life at that time. Its revival began during the Tang dynasty (618-907AD). In the late Tang, Confucianism absorbed some aspects of Buddhism and Taoism and was reformulated as Neo-Confucianism. In practice, however, the three doctrines of Confucianism, Buddhism, and Taoism were often melded together. The abolition of the Imperial Examination System in 1905 marked the end of official Confucianism. Chinese intellectuals were working hard to find a replacement to fill the vacancy. Communism was the choice for the Communist Party and the People's Republic of China.

The implication in today's modern life is that sons and daughters should take good care of their parents and grandparents. China has a national holiday called Tomb Sweeping Day (around April 5th, calculated by Chinese Lunar Calendar). This day is dedicated for Chinese to pay respect to their ancestors by visiting and cleaning their ancestors' tombs.

With China's increasing urbanization, Chinese family members are often being separated. Younger generations go to bigger cities looking for better careers, and older parents are left to stay in their hometown. Due to China's inadequate retirement plan and facilities for elderly citizens, this has caused increasing social problem for older citizens. Because of this, the government is enacting laws that demand sons and daughters go home to visit their parents every year.

Confucian values also gave birth to a Chinese meritocracy. The Confucian main basis of teaching was to learn self-regulation, seek knowledge, and study to become a better person, to take good care of one's own family. Another goal was striving to become a Junzi (君子). The Junzi were referred to as a class of social intellectual elites with nobility of virtue, rather than nobility of blood. As a Junzi, the utmost goal was to help the emperor better manage the country and make the world a better place. Confucian classics sketch out a life path for intellectuals, which include self-regulation, taking good care of one's own family, helping manage the country and lastly making the world a peaceful and harmonious place. (修身、齐家、治国、平天下).

Meritocracy led to the creation of the Imperial Examination System in China. This system allowed anyone, regardless one's social background, to pass an examination to become a government official. The person who scored highest might have an opportunity to become the son-in-law of an emperor. The system is called by many academics as China's fifth invention, along the other four inventions of paper, gun powder, the compass and printing. The examination system, which originated in the Han period (206BC– 220AD), was officially introduced in 622AD, and was officially abandoned on 1906. The examination strictly tested on Confucian classics. The system had been very impartial throughout Chinese history. It provided a means of social mobility for ordinary families. The system stressed the nobility of virtues and good scholarship rather than nobility of blood. Therefore the mindset of changing social status through schooling and education has been deeply embedded in Chinese society. This has created a culture of quest for merit and studying.

Today the Chinese College Entrance Examination System is considered somewhat as an extension of the old system. Each year all high school graduates in the nation spend three days in June taking unified examinations. The scores will determine what kind of schools the students are able to attend. The system is very different from the U.S. college entrance system. Every year the Chinese government selects civil servants through national examinations in both written and oral form. This is quite similar to U.S. Foreign Service Exams, but much more selective, intense and rigorous. The Civil Examination evolved to replace the ancient Imperial Examination System. Even the Chinese media calls it the National Examination (国考). In 2013 1.119 million people applied and took the exam,

48

competing for limited government positions. The overall rate between the number of persons who took the exam, and those who were accepted and given a government job, is 57:1. For some more selective positions, the ratio is as high as 8000:1.

For many Americans working for the government is not as attractive as it is to the Chinese. Working for the government has been the top choice of employment of college graduates for a long time in China, and carries prestige. Every year many of the most talented graduates choose to work for the Chinese government. Attractive benefits and employment stability offered by government jobs are one reason. The other reason has to do with the Chinese culture. As in ancient times, the best scholars who excelled in the Imperial Examination System were chosen to serve as government officials. This comes from the Confucian value of government work being the natural outlet for good scholars.

Failure is the mother of success.

失败是成功之母。

Confucian Politics

Confucius' political thought is based upon his ethical thought. This is illustrated by the leadership formula: "Sageliness Within, Kingliness Without", which means that people who cultivate themselves according to Confucian ethics and become a sage will automatically demonstrate their kingliness to the outside, and people will follow them voluntarily and wholeheartedly. The practice of ruling the country by moral rightness and benevolence is called the "Kingliness Way". This makes it possible to bring peace and prosperity to their people, uniting people harmoniously from other ethnicities, and defeating enemies soundly.

Using the governance of "Kingliness Way", China was able to develop the Imperial Tributary System, which shaped foreign policy and trade for over 2000 years in East Asia. The system was the symbol of China's imperial dominance in East Asia. Through the System, the smaller neighboring countries were called "tributaries". These included such countries as the former Korea, Tibet and Vietnam, who came to China to pay their tributes to Chinese emperors by koutou and gifts. In return, these tributaries would win China's protection and trading opportunities. Before 1840 all Europeans who wanted to trade with China had to go through this highly restrictive system. China did not know that Europe had been through industrialization, and that a new world order was dawning including the Treaty System. The emerging power, Great Britain, sought to be treated as an equal and to place relations between Britain and China on a rational and ordered basis.

Of course, China did not grant Britain the request. Great Britain was getting increasingly dissatisfied and frustrated with the Chinese regarding trading. Finally a war broke out between Britain and China. Britain, equipped with new technology and power through industrialization, was able to defeat China, and forced China to sign the Treaty of Nanking in 1842. The Treaty forced China to open up more markets and accept the Western treaty system. The signing of The Treaty of Nanking represented the end of Chinese dominance in East Asia, and the collapse of the Chinese Imperial Tributary System. From then on China descended to a semi-colonial country for the next 100 years. The intellectuals in the late nineteenth century and the early twentieth century blamed Confucianism for China's weaknesses.

In the West Christianity teaches the concept of original sin, that humans cannot be trusted, and they need rule of law to contain negative human tendencies. On the other hand, Confucius believed that Man is originally born good. Because of this the whole administrative system has been historically built based on this assumption of the people being good. This carries over into the way to lead and manage people, rather than ruling by law. Leadership emphasizes internal ethical disciplines, demonstrating leadership by good example. When a leader is found that he or she is not able to live up to the ethical standards, he or she loses the legitimacy of being a leader. If you lead correctly, orders are unnecessary and useless. If the people are led by laws, and uniformity gained by punishment, people will try to avoid the punishment, but they have no sense of shame. If they are led by virtue and uniformity based on the rules of propriety, they will have a sense of the shame, and moreover will become good. This sense of shame is about an internalization of duty, where punishment precedes the evil action, instead of following it in the form of laws.

A very important aspect of the hierarchical family or corporate family is to give due respect to superiors. Rather than imposing silence on inferiors, this actually demanded that the inferior must give advice to his superior if the superior was considered to be taking a course of action that was wrong. Of course this advice must be given within the context of high regard and respect for the leader, and in private so as not to challenge the public face of the leader. Therefore, in terms of execution, Chinese society is extremely effective, since they follow their leaders' decision very closely, and sometimes blindly.

Historically the ruler of a city or a province was considered the "Official like Father and Mother". The ruler would consider his territory as family, and the people living in his territory as ruler's family members. In today's China, even though the Chinese government is ruled by one party, it does not mean that it has only one voice. There are many voices internally. Each top leader will represent a different perspective and interest. Therefore, the top government leader needs to balance the power internally.

Today it is quite difficult for most Americans to understand how the Chinese government functions. The same holds true for Chinese to understand how the American democratic government works. For instance, most Chinese are puzzled about why the U.S. government shutdown occurred during the budget crisis in September 2013. From a Chinese perspective it is inconceivable to think of a Chinese government shutdown which would cause the nation's leader to be unable to participate in one of the most important meetings such as the APEC meeting which the U.S. President Barack Obama missed.

The Chinese government is a form of authoritarian structure, however it is has evolved from the pure communist dictatorship of the Mao Period from 1949 to 1976. Today's Chinese government is a collective leadership composed of seven leaders in the Standing Committee of the Political Bureau in Chinese Communist Party. Consensus needs to be reached on critical decisions. The Chinese Communist Party and government both have very robust rigorous leadership development, evaluation and promotion structure and process. It will be easy for Americans to understand how Chinese government functions by imagining if the United States were run by the Pentagon. All Chinese leaders are like generals in the military. They have been promoted through ranks by merit, and they have been through rigorous scrutiny during their ascendance. The Chinese government and Communist Party systems are extremely well organized and highly effective. In the past only a Communist Party member was able to be promoted to certain higher ranks. Now non-party members are able to be promoted to the minister level, which is unprecedented, and impossible even 20 years ago.

Many policies that the current Chinese government promotes have strong elements of Confucian values. One example is the "Chinese Dream" put forth by president Xi Jinping after he ascended to China's top leadership position in November 2012. The primarily goal of the Chinese Dream is a "great rejuvenation of the Chinese nation". He is calling for every Chinese to "dare to dream, and work assiduously to fulfill the dreams and contribute to the revitalization of the nation." This may sound vague and sloganeering to the American audiences, but Mr. Xi emphasized that China would definitely achieve the Chinese dream. There are three phases timetable which was outlined for achieving the Dream. The first phase has a target for completion in 2021. This will commemorate the 100th anniversary of Chinese Community Party. The goal of this phase is for China to have become a middle class country, with an average per capita income over USD $10,000, or a "moderately well-off society".

The second phase has a target date of 2049, which is the centennial of the founding of People's Republic of China. By this time China wishes to become a fully modern developed country. The third phase will be to achieve the great full rejuvenation of China with strength and prosperity for the rest of 21st century. Mr. Xi also stressed that the means of achieving the Chinese Dream has three "musts". The means must follow Chinese paths, must advocate Chinese Spirits, and must accumulate Chinese power. The Dream emphasizes that the personal dream is secondary to the collective bigger Dream. It is everyone's responsibility and duty to work hard and work together towards the renaissance and rejuvenation of China. The Chinese dream differs in that the American dream focuses more on an individual's right to live a more proper, fuller life, regardless of social background and circumstance of birth. The Chinese Dream, on the other hand, puts an emphasis on collective elements of the dream. It is a national dream and collective ambition.

When people are of the same mind, they can fill up the oceans and move the mountains.

(IN UNITY THERE IS STRENGTH.)

人心齐，海可填，山可移。

Confucius in Modern Social Context

The core of Confucian ethics means treating situations and decisions in a contextual manner. Within Chinese society this is not considered a double standard or integrity problem. Chinese people expect to be treated differently from each other. People interpret how you treat them to mean something, so it's highly important to have a local Chinese consultant on a U.S. management team to guide decisions that affect how people are treated. Boundaries are blurred sometimes at work. Many Chinese company leaders give a gift to their subordinates, so they might view the leader as a good friend.

Face is an important concept derived from Confucian ethics. The underlying meaning has to do with social status. Giving people face means lifting their social status, with a secondary meaning involving moral standards. These standards are roles and expectations created by Confucian ethics. When we say someone doesn't care about face, it means they don't care about moral standards. If someone says a leader has no face or doesn't care about face, it means they don't care about the intricacies of Confucian ethics, and they fail to understand the underlying social expectations and moral standards. In the U.S. this very same attitude may equate to equality and be considered a virtue.

Time is fluid in Chinese culture. Schedules are reprioritized based on what seems important in the present. If an appointment is made for next month, it may change when the time comes. Future plans aren't important, and may be forgotten. It's important to reconfirm and follow up all the time. Time in China is used in a flexible and contextual manner. If the plan is very important, people can be very punctual. If it's not perceived as important, people will be very flexible.

Being proactive and taking initiative is not always in the Chinese DNA. Children are rewarded for being obedient. Leaders have more freedom. They know their subordinates look up to them, so they can become more creative. They themselves have worked their way up through the hierarchy, and they have now become the father within the organization. They can now be autocratic and demanding because that is the expectation of their subordinates. Before they become a leader they're obedient, and after they become the leader their role changes.

Chinese philosophy is studied by everyone, and teaches how to become a good leader. A good leader understands the Chinese system. People practice being a leader before becoming a leader. The leader develops himself/herself, goes to school, and has a strong capability of teaching themselves. They gain information from Chinese literature, studying all of their lives and developing on their own. Some have also been educated in the U.S. or other Western countries. Some Chinese governments send high potentials to Singapore to learn their systems to help them develop into leaders.

Everyone fulfills their role in society. When Chinese workers are quiet it doesn't mean they don't have anything to say. It just means they're mindful of their place in society and they're trying to fulfill the role given to them. Before speaking up they prefer to have had time to consider carefully what they will say. Letting them know your expectations in advance is very helpful to them.

Relationships in the West are very specific. Personal and professional lives are more separate in the U.S. than in China. Westerners would ask colleagues less often to do personal favors for them, than the same situation in China. In China things get done through favor exchange.

Confucian ethics and other Chinese traditional values have been deeply suppressed since 1896, when China was defeated by the much smaller Japan. Japan had already successfully industrialized. In 1919 the "May 4th" Movement broke out among students and intellectuals who strongly advocated embracing Western principles of "Democracy and Science" to strengthen the country. The social elites and intellectuals attributed the weakness of country to Confucian and traditional values. During the Cultural Revolution (1966-1976), initiated by Mao Zedong, a quite total attempt was made to destroy Confucian ethics and Chinese traditional values. This created a vacuum of belief in China. When Deng Xianping initiated the open-door policy in late 1970s, China embraced Western values along with capitalism, to form so-called "Social Capitalism".

In the past several decades China has become more global and has developed its economy rapidly. On the other hand there has been a renaissance of Confucian ethics and traditional values in China. Business elites have returned to school in droves to study Confucian ethics and other traditional classics. In September 2013, the former spokesperson of China Ministry of Education, Mr. Shuming Wang, even advocated in his Weibo (the Chinese version of Twitter) the abandonment of English study in elementary schools, and instead suggested studying more Chinese traditional classics. This generated a great debate in the Chinese media.

Pure gold fears no fire.

(A PERSON'S TRUE CHARACTER IS REVEALED IN ADVERSITY.)

真金不怕火炼。

Role of Women in China

Historically in Confucian society, woman only had a role in the family, and literally no role in politics. This carried out the popular notion that men govern the outer world, while women govern the home. There was a four-character phrase throughout China's Imperial period ended in 1911. The four-character phrase means "Three Obediences/Subordinations and Four Virtues for Women". The content is translated as follows:

Three Obediences/Subordinations

Be obedient to father or elder brother before marriage.
Be obedient to husband after marriage.
Be obedient to sons when widowed.

Four Virtues

Morality means that women needed to obey the rules in society, and be loyal to husband and family. In the Ming dynasty (1368-1644AD), a tradition of virtuous widowhood developed. Widows, even if became a widow at a young age, would be expected not to remarry. Their virtuous names might be displayed on the arch at the entrance of the village. This was considered one of most important Morality for women traditionally.

Proper speech means encouraging women to be careful with words at all times, avoiding negative words which might stimulate conflict among family members, using positive words to encourage their husband, and using a more strict tone to discipline sons and daughters.

Modest Manner and Appearance means demanding women to have simple make-up, dress properly, and be tidy, should not be too sloppy in her appearance. Foot binding.

Diligent work means requiring women to work hard at home, learning all skills needed to take care of the family.

After 1911 China entered into a new world with radical social change and revolution, and started modernizing. The Three Obediences and Four Virtues toward traditional women were considered as spiritual restraint imposed on Chinese women. Many women stepped out of their families, going to schools, getting educated and learning new skills and contributing to the social development. Women's social status then greatly improved. After the founding of the People's Republic of China in 1949, one of country's key policies has been gender equality, echoed by Mao's famous slogan, "Women Hold Up Half of the Sky". This effort has been paid off, and has unleashed the power of women in modern China, particularly in Chinese cities. However, the goal has not been totally reached. Gender inequity is still a key social problem in China. Men still hold most of the key positions of power within the country in virtually all political, economic, bureaucratic, academy and military spheres.

Today Chinese women still face strong social pressure to marry before the age of 30. Parents, given the choice of one child, often prefer a boy, considering the traditional value of the male over the female. This has led to high number of sex-selective abortions of females in China. Currently, according to census data, China's sex ratio at birth was 108 males to every 100 females in the early 1980s, which was only slightly above the natural rate of 103 to 107. In 2000 the ratio was 116.9 males to 100 females, and in 2010 it was 118.08 males to 100 females.

In some provinces, such as Anhui, Jiangxi and Shaanxi, the sex ratio has soared to more than 130 males to every 100 female births.

It is not only a population problem, but also a grave social problem as many men will fail to find a wife. It's estimated that by 2020 China will have 24 million more men than women of marriageable age in China. In last half century China has made remarkable improvement in combating gender inequity. At present the majority of women work in China. The power of women has contributed a great deal to China's modern economic growth and social development.

Co-author Donny tells a story about a friend who is Korean-American and holds a Harvard MBA. She held a position as CFO for a large U.S. technology company in China. She told Donny her impression was that China was a much more female friendly country for a working woman than her home country of Korea. She said that it would probably not be possible to hold her current position if it were in Korea. Both Korea and Japan are both deeply Confucian influenced countries, however do not have the gender equity that China has achieved.

Today, many Americans will read news about China, and encounter Chinese people who are very different from what we describe here in our book. It is because China as a country is undergoing swift reform and change right now, transitioning toward a more developed and industrialized country from an old agricultural state. This is somewhat like the analogy of repairing and building a new facility in an old ship while it is sailing. The influence of Confucian ethics has been weakened in the last hundred years, while the rule of law has become a more effective mechanism, and has not yet been fully established. As a result, China is in between. The Chinese people who live in China today are facing huge challenges as they adapt to the new changes brought by the country's reforms. Each one may react to the environment differently. Therefore, people from outside China need to look at China and Chinese people both historically and holistically.

Without going through the severe cold of winter, one cannot appreciate the warmth of spring.

不经冬寒，不知春暖。

Confucian Ethics and Business

While Confucian morals and ethics are prevalent within Chinese business, the best illustration is Chinese private business. Probably most Americans may not know that there are over 10 million private corporations in China, which accounted for over 60% of Chinese GDP in 2012. The majority of these companies are family-owned. In China, family business is a business family. Many business are conducted through a network of trusted relationships.

For a foreign company the practice of running a Chinese business based on Confucian ethics may be unfamiliar. The best way to grasp these practices and demonstrate the distinctions between Chinese and American business practices is through the specific and detailed example of two people attending a cross-cultural training course. Let's say Jim and Wang are co-workers in a U.S. based multinational company opening a new office in Beijing. They are both new hires. Jim came from corporate headquarters located in the U.S., and Wang grew up in Beijing. One morning Jim arrived at his desk and noticed Wang has not yet come to work. Moments later he received a phone call from Wang asking Jim to please say he is there in case the boss asks for him. Wang explained that a pressing family issue has delayed his arrival.

What is each man thinking during this telephone interchange? Jim is thinking from a U.S. point of view where laws make punishments clear. He read in the employee handbook that anyone covering for someone else who is not doing their work could get in trouble, and would probably be given a warning which would stay in their personnel file. He doesn't understand why Wang would put him in this precarious position, and he feels very uncomfortable with Wang's request. Jim sees time as static. For him there is a set time to arrive and there are no excuses for not showing up at the appointed time.

Wang is thinking from a Chinese point of view where laws are applied within the context of a situation. He grew up studying classics, which involved reading about Confucius, then reflecting upon and discussing with his classmates how various Confucian ethics would apply within a range of situations. He remembers there is a duty to family before community, and he thinks of his co-workers as extended family. He expects his extended family to help him save face with the community, so it seems natural to ask for this favor of his co-worker. Wang knows the U.S. company expects him to arrive at a certain time, and he's balancing this with his cultural orientation. Time is fluid, and what is most important in the moment gains priority.

Western society is regulated by the rule of law. For 2,000 years the Chinese have been regulated by Confucian ethics, though now within China there are more and more conflicts emerging between Confucian ethics and the rule of law, as China moves toward a modern society. In the long run, rule of law will to some extent begin to co-exist with Confucian ethics in regulating society in China.

Gary observes one of the things he hears Western leaders complaining about is the lack of formal rules in China. A U.S. executive visiting China may think they have an agreement to build a factory, but nothing is written down. Their Chinese contacts say just go ahead and build the factory. This is difficult from the Western side, because their attorneys and shareholders want something signed with all the contingencies explicitly laid out before they invest resources into a new project. It appears from the Western standpoint there is too much of a gray area with everyone just feeling their way, and with fewer things written down than would be normal for the Westerner.

The Chinese may feel uneasy because they think if their Western contacts need every contingency figured out in advance, perhaps the Westerner does not trust them. From the Chinese point of view there is often an assumption made that we are all good and honest people, and that when there is trust, a solution will be found within the context of the situation. In a sense the Westerner is right—for the Chinese there is an element of feeling their way along. They reason that if they want to do the project, the Chinese will wish to just do it. This takes a big leap of faith from the Western point of view. Westerners are accustomed to protecting themselves legally from punishment. From the Chinese point of view, they only step in when someone does something wrong. At that point they step in with punishment, and then they have rules. Again to Westerners this sounds very precarious.

The U.S. has a system of definite rules and seems to think that life can be regulated with predictability. Chinese say everything is fluid, and it's the context at the moment of where you are that matters. Who can predict the future? Traditionally for the Chinese, the law is a supplement to ethics. Ethics are more important than the law. When there is a conflict between ethics and the rule of law, context comes into play. What is the right thing? Maybe the law says one thing, but ethics applied within context determines the outcome. From the Chinese point of view, what U.S. leaders do wrong is to base their rules on a specific situation. A remedy may work in one case, and it may not work in another situation. From a Western standpoint, the Chinese lack of rules, systems of timekeeping, and when and how decisions are made may seem ambiguous and arbitrary. From the Chinese point of view, the Western way of creating static agreements that are not flexible enough to allow for evolution and changes to occur may seem archaic and short sighted.

Decisions Among Friends

Donny tells a story about meeting a friend for dinner in Berlin. They first spoke briefly in his friend's office, then walked out of the university and found themselves facing a five star hotel. He told Donny, "If you were a Chinese government official, I would take you to the five star hotel. It's expensive and the food is not as good as other places, but it gives people face. You and I are good friends. Within walking distance there is a very good café which is very German. Which do you prefer, the five star hotel or the bar?" As friends they didn't need to think about giving each other face because they already had a trusting relationship with each other, so they chose the informal bar. The next level of decision was ordering food. Donny's friend said, "If you and I were not very close friends, I would order two dishes. But because the dishes are so large, and because we are close we can order one that we share." The contextual nature of Chinese culture is probably the most frustrating part for people outside of China to understand and learn.

Confucian ethics are grounded in basic and fundamental concepts focused on an emphasis of personal and governmental morality, social relationships, justice and sincerity. These crucial principles and values are the lifeblood of the Chinese business institution. To understand these important concepts is to gain the inside track into successfully practicing in the world of Chinese business.

Transforming oneself into a global leader takes time and effort. Most importantly, it takes the desire and passion to both understand and respect the differences between the two culturally accepted norms. Chinese politics, religion and moral obligations play an enormous role in the context of corporate governance and accepted business practices. In the next chapter we discuss the generational differences in Chinese society and offer insight into traditional Chinese views of society, family, and business.

Laughing one time can cure hundreds of illnesses.

(LAUGHTER IS THE BEST MEDICINE.)

一笑治百病。

© Can Stock Photo Inc. / Vyusur - Original art, watercolor painting of bamboo, Asian style painting.

Generational Differences in Chinese Society

Grooming a new generation of leaders is essential for any company or country. An exploration of a country's morals, characteristics, business, history, fundamental principles, and the context from which its leaders emerge will provide a more comprehensive understanding of the cultural environment. This chapter will help you learn more about how generational differences within Chinese society affect business and relationships. Just as different generations in the U.S. are associated with certain characteristics, so are different generations in Chinese society associated with certain characteristics. Understanding the environment that shaped Chinese employees within an organization can help U.S. leaders effectively match their expectations and initiatives to the individual. Consider the following generational delineations to better understand the generational mix in the Chinese culture:

Over Forty: Chinese who are now over 40 years old grew up during a period when China was a very oppressive society. People lived in poor villages with very few opportunities for education or the ability to improve their standard of living. They were taught to know their place and to bend to authority without question.

Over Thirty, Under Forty: Chinese who are over thirty but yet to reach forty years old began to see some changes as they grew up. They were still raised with the traditional values of obedience to authority, and may find it difficult to think for themselves unless they were some of the few who were able to study abroad.

Over Twenty, Under Thirty: Chinese who are over twenty but yet to reach thirty years old were born into the very different world of China's one child policy. While this reduced Chinese population growth, it also changed dynamics within Chinese families. Two parents and four grandparents now had only one child to focus on, and only one child now had the responsibility to support two parents and four grandparents later in life. As society changed in the past few decades, there was ever increasing competition for limited space in schools and universities. Because of this, focus on study became extremely important to children, more so than responsibilities in the home. Children were told their most important duty was to study, because of steep competition from other young people. They were the first generation in decades with such educational opportunities.

An understanding of these age and generational considerations can shed light on why both U.S. and Chinese leaders report that Chinese employees who were are over twenty years of age but under thirty are sometimes seen as more difficult to manage, but also carry the largest payoff to the team and to the organization as a whole. The twenty-something generation is the "new" generation of employees with an entirely unique set of values and needs never before seen in the general Chinese workforce. Managers often evaluate their maturity level as low. They sometimes seem very sensitive to criticism. Because of how they were brought up, they have a strong sense of entitlement. They are able to work independently but are not very collaborative. Some say the lack of collaborative skills comes from having no interaction as children with siblings. One HR leader describes a situation where a young employee cried because the boss had complimented two others in a meeting without complimenting this young person as well.

With the challenges come new possibilities. The younger generation also presents great opportunities to create an exciting work environment, as they are very ambitious about their own achievement within the company. They are eager to show their performance, and they are impatient to get promoted as soon as possible. This is generally the result of the notion that their experience in school taught them to excel as individuals, and to be very competitive. In a very practical way they need to achieve as individuals in order to support their parents and grandparents long term.

This younger generation continuously looks for new and better positions, so they seem to change jobs every 18-24 months. They know they're likely to get another increase in compensation if they leave their current job before 3 years, when they would normally get a salary increase in their current position. There is a "me first" attitude. They grew up as the only child with no siblings to share with. Their parents and grandparents doted on them. They have not have the need for developing social skills, they may appear more greedy to older generations, and in general expect more. High potentials are especially self indulgent and feel entitled. Bending the truth and rationalizing to get what they want or to save face often deviates from the moral compass of their grandparents. One leader advised, "If they say yes, put a contract in front of them and if they don't sign, they mean no."

(When shaking bottles)

The half filled ones make noise, and the fully filled ones are silent.

(THOSE WHO KNOW THE LEAST BOAST THE MOST, WHILE THE SUPERIOR PERSON REMAINS SILENT.)

一瓶不响，半瓶咣当。

The Chinese middle class is getting new economic power. There are more people with more money. Chinese college graduates in Chinese companies are increasingly able to command a compensation package that is roughly similar, whether they work in Chinese or Western companies in China. Those Chinese who have had Western education or Western professional experience are valued increasingly for their *global mindset*. It is still very attractive for Chinese youth to attend U.S. universities to learn about U.S. business methods and culture, and develop their *global mindset*. What is changing, is that although the Chinese youth sometimes chooses to study in the U.S., opportunities are often greater, including higher compensation, for the Chinese to return to China.

Not that long ago the majority of Chinese had no chance for higher education. They lived in villages with only basic amenities, and with few opportunities. Materially China has been improving exponentially in recent decades. Whereas in the past Chinese looked to Western multinationals as having most sought after positions, now some of the best and brightest choose to stay in China and work for Chinese State Owned Enterprise because jobs are more secure, and with the 'hidden benefits' the total compensation is much better than other options. 'Hidden benefits' are non-salaried perks.

People born who are now between 20-30 years old are sometimes called the 1980s generation. Because their living conditions and future prospects are so vastly different from their parents' and grandparents' generation, the 80s generation isn't as willing to subdue their own personal desires as their parents were. This sometimes creates conflict between the generations. The generation of the 80's are questioned by older generations. They see the younger generation as having a low tolerance of the environment and its surrounding pressure. The

73

80's generation tends to show less respect to authority with regard to the boss and leader, compared with those generations that are older.

The new generation of Chinese workers under thirty is seen to not take as much responsibility for their work as earlier Chinese generations. They change jobs more frequently and are constantly looking for a better environment and greater pay. Salary isn't as important as the environment. They have an extreme desire to improve. A better environment to them means more training opportunities. They live with anxiety about their level of improvement. They are worried that if they stay in the same place they will fall behind. Living in a dynamic society, they have to continue to be superior to others, so they value improving themselves.

The twenty-something generation demonstrates behaviors that are egocentric. This is a key factor to understand as it can bring advantages and disadvantages. Under Chairman Mao people could only obey, but the new generation thinks for themselves. They are more individualistic and more likely to focus on what is inside of their hearts, and what they truly want. They may see selfishness as an advantage.

Their parents tell them they should sacrifice now for later gain, but this new generation tends not to sacrifice. When they see something wrong with their society and leaders, they expect that they can change things as individuals and take responsibility in the long term. They know their parents and teachers lived in a depressed situation without opportunities for education. Their parents see the 80s generation as their future, so they want their children to complete college. Their first goal for their child is to get them into a university. The child may be ready to identify their career plan, but because their teachers grew up in a society where there was no such thing as a career plan, students aren't trained by their teachers in how to plan their professional future.

Even more exciting is that they have hope. They see themselves creating a life in the ashes of the great cultural revolution that destroyed the culture and morality of the Chinese people. They see all of China's current problems deriving from the shadow of the great cultural revolution. They find themselves in a position of having to invent their own way to survive in a very new and competitive world. The most authentic moral compass they can find is within their own hearts and desires. This may come across to older, more obedient generations as selfish and irresponsible, however it may be their only way to forge a viable path to the future.

If you are too greedy, you cannot chew sufficiently before you swallow.

(DON'T BITE OFF MORE THAN YOU CAN CHEW.)

贪多嚼不烂。

What the 80s Generation Wants

One member of the Chinese 80s generation told us what they want most is to achieve self value. They have to discover for themselves what this means. Generations before them lived lives obedient to authority, without the opportunity to explore personal fulfillment. Their teachers in school can't help them create a career plan, because this has not been part of Chinese society earlier generations. They are the generation that carries hope for the many generations before them. They care about self-improvement to support their future potential for promotion at work, which in turn will help them support their family, and their parents and grandparents.

Even with all of this pressure to perform, some choose with their heart and become artists and accept other lower paid occupations. These people often know their choice will likely leave them without the means to support a family, and may create financial limitations within their extended family. Some would prefer to become artists, but choose a corporate career because they need money to survive and thrive in society. The value of a Chinese artist is to explore the spiritual realm instead of the money realm. Older generations had only one choice for their career, and it was very difficult to get into a university or college. The many choices and pressures in today's Chinese society can sometimes tempt young people to become more motivated by greed.

Generational Differences

Historic changes such as the Chinese reform and the opening-up policy in 1979 resulted in the population becoming wealthier. Western culture has had more influence on the Chinese culture during the past few decades. To Chinese living with so many limitations from the past, Western movies, news and television seemed like heaven. This was very different from the older generation's experience. The accompanying opportunities for higher education, advancement, and technology were very welcome. Laws are changing in China. The availability of the Internet has made efficient communication possible. People are able to express more of their true feelings and desires through Weibo and other Chinese social media. The government has allowed more freedom of speech.

Some in Chinese society recommend the 80s generation youth work in a U.S. company because a U.S. company tends to emphasize more training. Financial goals are all important to this generation. China's tax rates are high, and yet their citizens often don't see the money coming back to them in the form of a social safety net. Housing is among the most expensive in the world, and people pay for their own medical expenses. Competition is high on every front.

One young man reported housing prices puts even more strain on the 80's generation because of what he called stacking. By the time a man is 30 years old he needs a house in order to get married. At this point he is also responsible for his parents, and his wife's parents. Because of the one child policy there are now four parents to be supported by only two people. The grandparents will provide childcare for grandchildren, but this whole experience doesn't allow him to enjoy life or save money. He must be very serious and focused on continuous training and career improvement to stay ahead of the competition.

77

Some of the most promising university graduates in China today choose a career path with the government or a State Owned Enterprise. There is often a supplement to the salary in State Owned Enterprises in the form of 'hidden welfare' or 'grey income'. This may be in the form of gift cards for groceries and other benefits that are above and beyond the basic salaries. When all of this compensation is taken into consideration, people feel they are getting as much monetary compensation as the Western multinationals pay, and the government or State Owned Enterprises are seen to be more secure. They don't the same reputation for hiring and firing people as Western multinationals. This has caused reduced interest in U.S. companies in the long term because of Western limitations. There are more limited opportunities for promotion with U.S. companies, and everything including salary is standardized. Standardized procedures mean less negotiating room for salaries. In the less fixed Chinese system, it's possible to get a much higher salary depending on relationship ability ('relationship ability' means the quality of one's relationship with the government and leaders). As a result the money is better in a Chinese company, but training is better in a U.S. company.

From the 80's generation perspective, Western multinational companies provide some important advantages, including a broader experience and valuable training. Knowledge of how U.S. companies organize processes and work flow with standard operating procedures is valued. Bringing that knowledge back to China is seen to improve a young person's chances of getting a good government position. China is only beginning to implement such organizational practices.

Without clearly defined job responsibilities, blame can become a more prevalent factor in the Chinese workplace. This can come in the form of more time lost debating and discussing issues, with a strategy of pushing off the work to other departments that may operate in the same or similar area of responsibility. There is always some form of debate during a project. Chinese work relationships can be more complicated because of underlying issues and unclear, competing boundaries. Employees cannot always say what they want. They may be thinking, "I hate you but I won't tell you. I'll organize my group against you." In the U.S. debate occurs before a rule is formed. Time is taken in advance to discuss related issues and recommended courses of action, so when the decision is made the rule is followed and enforced. In China a company is formed without rules. Debate occurs during the process of execution. Rules are developed during the work process, and are focused on a very practical level of getting things done step by step as work moves towards the goal.

Large U.S. companies train their employees on international standards and ideas, leadership concepts, technical methods, and professional skills based on current industry standards. Chinese companies don't do this as well, because they don't have a previous generation of well educated, skilled trainers. Chinese are still in the beginning phases of their industrial revolution.

Understanding the motivational factors involved with new generation employees will provide insight from which to motivate young people and inspire loyalty to the company. One young Chinese man recommended the following steps to a successful working relationship with his generation:

- Let the young employees know they are improving.
- Let them know what future they can expect.
- Give them compliments and suggestions for improvement.

Chinese workers are not afraid of pressure, but after the project is completed they need to hear praise for improvement. Providing them with learning opportunities, such as making presentations, to help them improve their skills, will be appreciated. Much like in the U.S., Chinese workers value and appreciate constructive feedback with the notion that they will be celebrated for their victories. Creating a team mentality will allow employees to flourish and grow, providing better results and more success for the business as a whole. Through structure and well organized opportunities to grow, it is possible to bridge the generational gap and utilize the strong qualities this new age of employees can bring to the table.

As a globally minded leader with the goal of building a business in China, what does this mean for you? The short answer is that a strong leader understands the motivators for those they lead. Maximizing the team's effort to ensure they reach goals and work in an optimal manner is the same task for any leader whether in China or North America. The manner in which these goals are reached, and the approach made to the employees when providing direction, may be very different. One similarity between both China and North America is that twenty-something talent is beginning to encompass a larger percentage of the overall workforce. They bring with them motivators and expectations different from many in previous generations, so to bring the best out in them may require some different talent management strategies.

If you cannot behave yourself, how can you try to moralize others?

(WE SHOULD WORK ON MAKING OURSELVES BETTER INSTEAD OF TRYING TO IMPROVE OTHER PEOPLE.)

不能正己，焉能化人。

Cultural Dimensions

This chapter discusses concepts Donny Huang uses in his WordPass Cultural Assessment, which is used to measure cultural differences. Donny also finds this helps people to develop cultural self-awareness, and to reconcile and capitalize on the cultural differences. All cultural dimension concepts are based on the research of Dutch scholars Geert Hoftsede and Fons Trompenaars, except the Equal and Contextual dimension, which is intended to describe Chinese who often treat insiders and outsiders in vastly different ways.

Person to Person

Orientation: Equality and Status
Do you see everyone as equal, or do you pay close attention to status?

Let's say you're a leader whose base culture is Western, and you're now in China managing a local team. One of the tasks on your schedule today is to promote a local charity and solicit donations from your employees.

From your experience in the West you might expect that each person in the department will contribute whatever their individual conscience and budget will bear. You may not know that the hierarchical orientation in China affects even how much an employee will donate to a worthy cause. Nobody dares to donate over than the $1,000 their leader donated, because they think even donations are hierarchical. If you donate more, then you're asserting that you have higher power, so everyone is careful to stay within their culturally prescribed place.

Donny tells a story of 53 leaders in his classroom from a famous Chinese oil company. He asked the group, "How many of you are happy if your subordinate donates more than you?" Only one person raised their hand. One workplace implication of this dynamic is that Chinese employees will not proactively make decisions unless their boss tells them to do something specific. From a Western perspective, this puts too much pressure on the person at the top. Bosses are not perfect, so they can make a mistake. If no one is willing to challenge them, a bad mistake may not get corrected.

Western leaders often complain about Chinese employees not making decisions. It's important for Western leaders to understand the Chinese are actually very capable. They're simply afraid their boss doesn't want them to make decisions.

Providing clear directions and expectations, and enough time for the Chinese employee to consider options before making the decision, will create an environment more likely to get a helpful response from the Chinese employee.

Identity: Individual and Group
Are you more focused on the individual, or the group?

In Chinese society many decisions are made not from the perspective of the individual, but rather on what's best for the group. For example, if you ask students in a school how many of them chose this school and major by themselves, you'll find very few. Parents and even teachers chose the school for them. Decisions are made as a collective, and even the decision of school and career are not made from the individual's perspective.

Back to the earlier concept of hierarchy, even though the boss has the most authority in terms of making decisions, he still has many stakeholders and contingencies he has to consult in order to gain consensus before he makes this decision. These stakeholders may be his mentors or another agency. In order to maintain harmony and authority he will have individual meetings with stakeholders to work out any differences before he goes public with any statement. In this way the group is in a sense making the decisions.

From a Western leader's perspective everything is about the individual. The leader is responsible and accountable for the decision. Chinese society is like a collective of small families patterned after a traditional Chinese family. Family isn't composed of independent individuals. Donny gives an example. For instance let's say Donny wants to buy a house. He doesn't have enough money so he goes to his family. The decision is not about the person. Donny would have to ask his parents, their good friends, and insiders to make a good decision.

In the Western world after age 18 you're responsible for your own decisions, and parents' authority and responsibility end. It isn't that way in China.

In China if you go against the group intelligence, it's tough, but there are some ways around this. Let's say a Chinese man refuses to go to school where he was accepted, and where his parents had decided he would go. His parents would be upset with him, but if the decision would benefit his career, it could be accepted by them as a good decision. It's easier in many ways for Chinese people to go along with group intelligence as the mainstream. The underlying motive of the group is to help the individual become a good student, in order to become more successful in life.

Many Western leaders note the Chinese are diligent and work hard, but lack emphasis on creative thinking. They seem to focus more on rote learning such as memorizing facts. Western leaders often find themselves yearning for their Chinese staff to think outside of the box, and to come up with creative solutions. Coaching and cross-cultural training can be useful to help Chinese to not just be smart but be able to use the intelligence to develop other conditions and decisions. This training can be very useful to help those from a Chinese based culture to work cross culturally, preparing them for life outside of China. It's also important for Western leaders to learn how to manage a Chinese team.

Many Chinese leaders look at what may seem to them as tedious, wasteful conversation and negotiation by Western teams just to make incremental progress in a project. In the Chinese world, when a decision is made, execution is very fast and effective because nobody questions the decision. Everyone in the hierarchy below the leader just executes their portion of the project. This is how the Chinese can build vast, modern cities from nothing in a mere fifteen years. It sometimes takes that long to simply gain enough political support in Western cities to begin building.

Communication: Direct and Indirect

Do you look for subtle cues to decode in order to understand the message, or do you look for a direct answer to a direct question?

Chinese communication style as a whole is very indirect. Chinese is a high context culture, where communication is done through contexts. A Chinese person won't give you a lot of information if the relationship hasn't been developed first. Once the relationship has been developed, they become very direct. For example, Donny talks of staying with a U.S. family. In the morning he heard the husband and wife get up and say "Good morning, Honey." In China the first words may be in the imperative form "Make breakfast", or "Take the children to school".

In China if you are known as a friend you may get a very direct message. In the West even if you know the person well, you still treat them with respect, so you still say please and thank you. In China you have an assumption of the relationship. Chinese hear these more formal, respectful comments between close family members and may wonder, "Is the Westerner insecure in their relationships?" Westerners wonder why Chinese become so rude all of a sudden, not realizing it's a term of endearment! Another reason a Westerner may receive a direct message is that when their boss talks to them as a subordinate, it's done in the form of a very direct message.

Donny always encourages a new Western leader to understand the person's life first and build the personal connection. Later the employee will be more helpful to give the leader more inside information. If the leader doesn't have the connection and trust first, they probably won't feel safe enough to tell the leader the whole truth.

The biggest problem a Western leader faces when managing Chinese is expecting equality and democracy, and wondering why they are not willing or able to criticize and share creative thoughts in a public situation. Any of these behaviors will reduce trust with Chinese co-workers and leaders.

Taking direct, constructive criticism publically is very challenging for Chinese. Westerners aren't as defensive about this as the Chinese, because in the U.S. there is a long tradition of questioning authority. Upper mid level Chinese working in multinational organizations can find public feedback very difficult, because from their perspective it brings their authority into question. Face is very important to the Chinese. An essential aspect of the Western coaching process involves 360 assessments. In China it is especially important to do these 360 interviews in private.

Another aspect of face comes into play when an executive from one company meets with an executive from a Chinese organization. If the meeting is with a government official, it is advisable to first find out their status within the hierarchy, and then bring someone with corresponding ranking from your company with you to the meeting. Treat the Chinese leader with respect. It may well be worth the expense of setting up a government relationship division which does all the work for you. You as the leader can simply support their efforts until they let you know they need you at a meeting.

Chinese Communication Style is somewhat contextual:

- Boss to Subordinates: Direct.
- Subordinates to Boss: Mostly Indirect unless they are close as friends.
- Close Friend to Close Friend: Direct.
- Peers to Peers: Mostly indirect unless they are close as friends.

Consideration: Equal and Contextual

Do you treat others based on the rules, or within the context of a situation?

Chinese communication style is contextual and Chinese treat insiders and outsiders very differently. For instance, because I know you and like you, I have the right to joke with you and perhaps even seem to abuse you. It's a style of a friendship in China. Attention to formality until the relationship is created is important. If you meet someone you don't know, the interaction will be very much on the surface. If you meet someone at a higher level of authority, it's traditional to be obedient, use their title, and be very polite. If the person is at a lower level of status or a client, politeness is also very important. If you know the person, or if the person is senior to you but is a good friend, you can be very direct. It has more to do with the depth of relationship than level of hierarchy. However level of hierarchy is very important if the person is not a close friend. In China almost everything is contextual.

It takes time to build these relationships, and in Chinese companies where people stay in the same company for their entire career, this works. In Western companies where high

**When two tigers tussle,
one of them will get injured for sure.**

**(WHEN TWO POWERFUL PEOPLE COME INTO
CONFLICT WITH ONE ANOTHER, AT LEAST ONE
WILL GET SERIOUSLY HURT.)**

两虎相争，必有一伤。

Two tigers can't live on the same mountain.

**(TWO STRONG PERSONALITIES IN THE SAME
PLACE WILL ULTIMATELY CLASH.)**

一山不容二虎。

(Beware of) a tiger with a smile on its face.

**(YOU CAN'T TRUST A POTENTIALLY DANGEROUS
PERSON SIMPLY BECAUSE HE IS SMILING AT
YOU.)**

笑面虎。

90

potential leaders are transferred in and out of various positions rapidly, they don't have the same benefit of time in order to create these trusting relationships.

Chinese do not wish to enter into an agreement unless they feel they can trust and have a relationship. Westerners enter into relationships with people they don't trust because they think they've tied it up legally. They're more pragmatic. They're willing to go into business with enemies because from their experience, the law keeps everyone in line.

When new American expatriates take an assignment in China, it's best for them to wait before making most decisions. It works best to get to know the people first. Take them out to a meal. Build a personal relationship with the team first, rather than using the company's rules and regulations to enforce decisions.

Building a good relationship with Chinese is not an easy task. For example, Donny's German friend, who has been coming to China since the 1970s, brings small German gifts with him when he comes to China. In response his Chinese friends feel very good and he's perceived as very caring about them. He understands how to treat Chinese contextually. This custom of treating insiders and outsiders so differently can create problems for Chinese in the eyes of Westerners. Chinese risk being perceived as somewhat unethical by their Western counterparts. In Western contexts, people are encouraged to treat everyone equally and fairly.

Person to Business

Focus: Task and Guanxi
Would you prefer to do something quickly that might offend others, or do things more slowly in a way that won't offend others?

Most Western people are primarily focused on task. Most Chinese don't feel comfortable being so aggressive to get things done, and so careless about other people's feelings. The Asian style is to maintain harmonious, good relationships with everyone. When Westerners get things done under pressure, they often offend Chinese people without realizing it. From the Chinese point of view, pushing about the task without consideration of peoples' feelings is Western, and does not show proper respect for, or build relationship trust, with the Chinese.

Gary reflects that as Westerners we talk about how we value feelings, individuals, how they are to be treated, what they think ... and yet we also push them. Looking from the outside seems like two very different, opposite things we do at the same time. Westerners are very demanding but also think of themselves as attentive.

Another seeming dichotomy from the Western point of view is that on the street Chinese people appear to be very aggressive. People on the street push each other, not considering the other person at all. If a subway door opens, everyone pushes to get in. One Chinese man explains, "On the street, when I know you I have to be very careful. If I don't know you I can push and abuse you." Westerners hear how competitive Chinese society is to get into school, into a job, and how fierce the competition is, so that a Chinese person seems to know they have to push to get where they want to go. To the outsider this seems contrary to the public good.

Chinese businesses and management are more like a family. In China when you get things done you work with people who know you. Chinese can be very competitive if they don't know you. There is an inside and outside, and people are treated differently based on their place within or without the group. If you want to get things done inside the organization, you don't push people around. There is a desire for harmony and respect when you know each other.

Can multinationals operating in China create a sense of family? Can expatriate bosses trigger this family response in the staff? Can a multinational create a family dynamic? Chinese tell us this skill can be taught. There are some expatriates who understand this and can create a cohesive team. As discussed earlier, take your time. Don't make decisions right away. Get to know the people first. Take them to a meal. You need to get to know your people before you ask them to accomplish a task.

There is a new breed of middle class people in China who are much more individually oriented than the traditional culture. They are entrepreneurial, very aggressive and they want material success based on individual achievement.

Decision-making: Fact and Intuition

When making decisions do you tend to use a scientific method, or listen to your inner voice, paying attention to people's feelings?

If you ask a Chinese person how he or she makes a decision, whether it is fact-based or intuition-based, most likely the answer is: intuition-based. It will be easy to find that your Chinese colleagues and clients have a tendency to be judgmental and opinionated. Donny believes that this has something to do with the Chinese thought process and thinking pattern, which stems from the Chinese culture and educational system.

Historically in China, education was more about learning the right materials, and then writing essays expressing one's points of view. This can be seen in China's famous Imperial Examination System that many academia refer to as China's fifth invention. China's Imperial Examination System was officially established in 622AD, and was largely abandoned in 1906, but the origins of the system lie in the Han period (206BC-220AD). Throughout history, the content of the exam system remained remarkably constant. The core texts consisted of the Four Books and the Five Classics, works attributed to Confucius and some of his disciples, along with a number of approved commentaries. The examination system is still somewhat in use today. In Gao Kao, the China National College Entrance Examination, which is administrated 2-3 days every year, students are tested on designated content. Today, every year the Chinese government selects its civil servants through a similar national examination system, called Gong Wu Yuan Examination. The Western scientific fact based empirical research thinking pattern didn't come to China until very late, and even today there are few top Chinese scientists in mainland China. The only Chinese Nobel prize winners who won the prize did so after studying in the U.S.

Confucian ethics plays a major role in decision making. Chinese culture is deeply shaped by Confucian ethics, which has laid out many rules and behaviors that people should follow. Therefore, in Chinese daily life they internalize those ethics, and use those principles to guide themselves and judge others' behaviors.

An example would be a different approach between Eastern and Western medicine. A visit to a U.S. eye doctor would result in the doctor addressing the issue with the eyes. A visit to a Chinese doctor would go deeper by touching patient's pulse to decide what is wrong. Maybe a liver issue caused the eye problem. They look at the whole system. The U.S. system is more fact based, where each medical symptom is treated separately. There is an important place for both approaches in healing.

Western language and concepts cannot truly explain the Chinese medical system with their 5,000 years of history. Many things that exist in China can't be explained in English because the concepts are Chinese.

Locus of Control: Internal and External

Do you pay more attention to your personal willpower to push achievement forward, or do you pay more attention to conditions in the environment, patiently accepting and waiting for a favorable time to move forward with less effort?

Americans are more internally centered, owning both their mistakes and achievements. The thinking is, "If I try hard I can achieve". It's more focused on individual internal locus of control, thinking I can alter my life and environment, placing a value on continuous improvement. For instance, Western thinking leads to reliance on agricultural chemicals to overcome the environment and alter nature. Westerners look to empirical evidence for proof.

Chinese are more externally centered, saying it doesn't matter how hard I work if the environment doesn't allow me to succeed. Internal efforts are seen as a waste, as part of the game but not the whole game. Chinese are extremely sensitive to external factors, placing a value on acceptance and patience. Chinese thinking leads to accepting external conditions and working with the environment as it is, waiting for another change to occur. Chinese look to intuition and external conditions for guidance.

For example, Donny explains, the facts tell me I should make this decision, but how I feel, my intuition or intent, tells me to do something else. If my fate tells me I shouldn't do it, and I do it and I'm defeated, the consequences are compounded, so it takes longer to recover. If my fate tells me it's okay and I make a mistake, then my faith also tells me my moment hasn't yet come. If I had done it sooner there may have been more damage. This decision making becomes a blend of listening to my inner voice and understanding the external situation. The Chinese say wait for your moment to come. Watch for flow and tendency, so then you can achieve with less effort. Sometimes not doing anything is doing something. Wait for the right time, the right moment. Success is not based on pure effort, but on right time, right effort, right person. Patience.

Person to Time

Scheduling: Inflexible and Flexible
Do you start the day expecting your planned schedule to dictate how you focus your time and attention, or do you re-allocate your time based on the importance of needs as they occur during the day?

In the U.S. time and schedules are seen as a contract. When I make an appointment, it's an appointment. If I've made an appointment with someone and my circumstances change, or it looks like I'm going to be late, courtesy dictates that I inform the person I'm intending to meet, so they can alter their schedule. It's very rude and inconsiderate to simply not show up at the appointed time.

In China time proceeds differently. Most Chinese will allocate time based on present priorities. For example, Donny mentions an experience when a German client wanted to make an appointment with a Chinese government official. The German businessman made arrangements months in advance to get an appointment in the official's calendar. The message came back from the official's office confirming the appointment.

However, when the German client showed up in the Chinese government official's office, the official was not there. The German businessman was very frustrated, saying the Chinese official was not honest by not keeping his promise. Because he wanted to do business with the Chinese, he reluctantly rescheduled the meeting for a couple months later, making the necessary time in his own schedule, travel arrangements and the like in order to accommodate this change. When he returned for this second meeting, the Chinese government official was again unavailable.

If you want to catch a big fish, you should cast a long wire.

(TO GET SOMETHING BIG, YOU HAVE TO HAVE A LONG-TERM PLAN.)

放长线，钓大鱼。

Donny listened to this man's experience and suggested the German businessman contact the Chinese official by phone in the moment. Perplexed, the German businessman did so with a surprisingly positive result. The Chinese official saw this as important in the moment and made room in his schedule to meet with the German businessman on the spot.

Multinational companies are often very precise. Punctuality and sticking to agreements is a strong value. Western executives from the multinational may think they have a meeting set up, then at the last minute when they call to confirm the Chinese say, no, we're not ready to have the meeting. This can create confusion and lack of trust in the minds of the Western executives.

In a Chinese office if the boss calls in the morning with a new agenda, any previous commitments are forgotten in favor of the current priority. To Westerners this seems like a very disorganized way to operate. To Chinese it's more effective because they're doing what's most important at the time. They do have a plan, but they allow for a zigzag as the environment changes.

How to Boost Your Global Mindset

There are many ways to increase your ability to interact effectively in cross cultural situations. It starts with understanding who we are, our personality and our core cultural values. It means asking ourselves, "What does it mean being an American?", or "What does it mean being Chinese?" By understanding ourselves, it will help to set aside preconceived notions and judgments, and to become more receptive to different ways of thinking, communicating, managing and leading.

As a coach we might ask you to consider your own ways of doing things long enough to see more objectively where your own preconceived notions might be coming from. From that point of view, you may be able to see more clearly what's going on with the other person. Pay attention when you feel discomfort. Look deeper into your response, with a mind open to learning something new. You'll probably find greater understanding of the new culture, and gain new knowledge. This will help to build trust between Americans and Chinese, and how to communicate effectively between the two nationalities. After acquiring this knowledge, you will extend yourself by developing new principles which allow you to interact effectively with people from different cultures.

The hardest part of everything is always in the beginning.

万事开头难。

Applying Global Mindset to Your Global Venture

Before going to the other country, a U.S. or Chinese leader should consider the following:

1. What is your organizational objective in going to China?

2. What is your personal objective?

3. With that in mind, how can you experience organizational effectiveness by implementing Chinese elements into your objective? Look at Chinese values and corporate values. How can you address differences?

4. On the personal side, think about how to develop trust and your social support in Chinese society. Think about how Chinese society functions. Consider how to build personal friends in China.

It's also important to understand how the business model works in your industry in China. The environment is different than where you come from. For instance, China has strong government control, so dealing with government control in all regions is a very important part of your job. You may not learn this in the U.S. because government has less involvement with individual businesses, so you will need to learn new skills when operating in China. In addition, Chinese consumers are different from U.S. consumers.

- The business model in the U.S. is largely dependent upon rule of law and the ever-changing whims of consumers.

- Chinese and U.S. motivators are different. U.S. employees may respond to incentives they can earn as an individual, whereas Chinese employees may only respond to incentives they can earn as a team or a group.

- Family is very important to Chinese, so creating something to help them have face in front of friends and family can be very important.

Education is a key value in China, so sending Chinese employees to different educational programs can be a very strong motivator. Overseas training programs can be especially attractive.

Don't cross the river before rolling up your trouser legs. Don't open your mouth before you know the entire situation.

不挽裤脚不过河，不摸底细不开腔。

© Can Stock Photo Inc. / Elwynn - Chinese painting of plum blossoms.

Context and Rules

With fundamental historical and culture practices in mind, now comes the time to offer a more in-depth look at the context and rules that provide the groundwork for Chinese businesses. In any walk of life, we work under specific assumptions that often guide and lead us in a given direction. In business, we form these assumptions based on experience and consistent business practices. As you transition to working with Chinese companies, you will quickly find they work under an entirely different set of assumptions than those commonly practiced in America.

As one seasoned U.S. executive working in China said, the biggest issue between the West and China is that our starting assumptions are very different. Some of the largest distinctions between Chinese and American culture are:

Government: The form of government is probably the biggest difference between China and U.S. China has adopted an authoritarian form of government structure, with one party rule. Government has central control over many aspects of society. In China the government owns all of the land. All

105

property is leased from the government with a 70 year term. While the U.S. chooses a democratic form of governance, the society is mainly regulated by rule of law. Land ownership relies on 1,000 years of British law which says if you own land you can transfer it and develop it, according to applicable laws.

Regulations: In China it's best to assume you will need approval for many things. China has a strong government that lays down many regulations and these function as laws do in the U.S. In the U.S. approval is only needed if required by law. In the U.S., unless there is a specific requirement, landowners are free to do whatever they want. In China approval from the appropriate government agencies is negotiated with the appropriate authorities from those agencies, and decisions are context based.

Laws: Historically in China laws and rules were supplementary to Confucian ethics. Rules and laws were used to punish those who failed to fulfill their ethical responsibilities. In the U.S. having prior knowledge of the governing laws is key to building a successful enterprise. In China having good personal relationships with the appropriate people at the appropriate agencies is key to building a successful enterprise.

Growth: In the U.S. roads and infrastructure have been established for many decades, and laws concerning ownership and use of land have remained relatively stable during that time. In contrast, entire mega-cities have been built in China in a very short period of time, taking the local population from poor farmers to wealthy middle class city-dwellers in less than two decades.

Many Americans puzzle about why China has been able to grow so fast in last three decades. The main reasons are that, before 1979 economic reform, the Chinese economic structure was patterned on the state-planned economy of Russia. Under this form of state controlled structure, China struggled to manage growth. Deng Xiaoping, the architect of 1979 reform, introduced knowledge of free market capitalism. He called it Chinese Social Capitalism. Thus, he reorganized the importance of production in China according to capitalism. He integrated into the world supply chain the Chinese competitive advantage, which was cheap and hard working labor. As a result, China became the world's factory, which has enabled China's growth at a unprecedented rate.

Environmental Health: As a rapidly developing nation, China requires a tremendous amount of resources, sometimes with resulting pollution and environmental cost that would be punishable by law in the U.S. In the U.S. consumer sentiment is increasingly focused on protecting the environment. From the Chinese point of view, they're at a very different phase in development than the U.S. They see that the U.S. made many environmentally disastrous decisions during their earlier phase of development, which helped them develop more quickly. China's rapid growth has taken its toll on the environment. Smog and pollution are at dangerous levels in many large cities such as Beijing and Shanghai. In past few years China has embarked on a series of policies for environmental health, such as heavy investment in alternative energy, closing low value added factories, and limiting private car activities in big cities.

It should be clear how culture and general practices differ in China when compared with other parts of the world, particularly the United States. From the Chinese culture's view of growth, to the use of resources, legal and governmental regulations, the distinctions and cultural practices are significantly different. However, two of the largest variances, and probably the most important to business practices, would be how China views contractual relationships and corporate governance.

Contracts

Contracts are the backbone of American business. They outline responsibilities, exchange of monies, and the details that comprise any business relationship. In essence, nothing occurs in America without a contract as a foundation. The U.S. views contracts as a mechanism for protection, comfort, and understanding of mutual obligations. U.S. companies often feel nervous without contracts that lock down all contingencies. Chinese officials may feel offended when they are not trusted at their word, and concerned that they're not given latitude to maneuver as conditions evolve over time.

How can a static contract effectively support an enterprise when the only constant is change? Westerners face the challenge of obtaining a proper legal contract while taking into consideration Chinese culture and law. In addition, building adequate personal relationships in China is the key to success in the region. When involved in conflict in China, court should be considered the last resort. This is where relationships built with business and government officials may prove crucial to success. In China conflict with your partner needs to be avoided. In publicly announcing conflict with ones partner you are announcing that you are involved in an antagonistic relationship with your partner. Once this enemy relationship is established, it is difficult to reverse.

In the U.S. a contract is legal and binding, and puts forth responsibilities that are set in stone. Attorneys go through details with a fine toothed comb, considering all conditions which might possibly occur, and cover all contingencies with corresponding remedies. However, China is different. In China contracts are considered more a memorandum of understanding at the time. Terms and conditions can change, and are expected to change as circumstances change. Chinese feel superior to the West because as the world changes, it seems very impractical to lock people into an inflexible contract. The only way to alter a U.S. contract is to come to the end or to break it.

Because China is growing so fast, all aspects of Chinese governance are also in flux. Local governing bodies often create laws that conflict with each other, and in any case may not be current with new circumstances. Chinese people don't expect to always follow the rules, and enforcement of laws in China is nebulous and context based. Goals are accomplished through relationships, and society is based on harmony, so negotiations with U.S. attorneys can come across as abrasive and fickle.

People who grew up in the U.S. prize honesty, feeling there's a value in sharing information. From an Asian angle, it's more important to keep relationships harmonious. Keeping details less defined gives everyone more latitude for gradual change. If you're brutally honest, all things are on the table all of the time. If you're Chinese you're thinking about harmony rather than conflict, and also about greater maneuverability. You try not to ask yes or no questions, especially about important issues.

When negotiating a contract with a government agency, a representative from the foreign company and a representative with a corresponding level of authority from the Chinese government agency will sit down and talk about what they want. The first meetings will likely be focused on building mutual trust during a social event. Conversation will be about family, background, and personal experience with the goal of developing rapport. It would be respectful for the American to ask the Chinese person questions about themselves first, giving them the first opportunity to speak. After trust has been established, finally conversation will turn to the business at hand. In a respectful way, each party talks about what they want. The government representative may nod their head and make other signs of agreement, and may even write down what has been agreed upon during the conversation. The Westerner may go away from the meeting feeling relieved and happy about their successful negotiation.

However, they will soon learn this is only the beginning of the negotiation. The government representative may have made signs of agreement, however that positive response may have had a wide variety of meanings. It could have simply meant, 'Yes, I hear you.' It may have meant, 'I agree with you and I'm going to my leader with your requests and see what I can do.' In any case, it's likely someone in higher authority within the government will actually be making the decisions for the government agency.

When an official contract is finally signed in the U.S., it means all contingencies have been nailed down in detail, so later on if one party deviates from the details in the contract, the other party can take the matter to court and enforce the details outlined in the contract. When an official contract is finally signed in China, it means each party has outlined their best thoughts about how they can proceed based on current conditions. It is assumed adjustments will be made in the future as conditions evolve. The presence of trusted relationships between parties is of utmost importance for success long term. Contracts in the U.S. are often between parties who don't particularly trust each other, but who do trust the law and their contract to protect them.

What you do not want to be done to you, do not do to others.

(DO UNTO OTHERS WHAT YOU WANT TO BE DONE TO YOU.)

己所不欲勿施于人。-Confucius

Corporate Governance

The other imperative piece of the Chinese business industry that offers glaring differences with common American business practices is corporate governance. In a simplistic framework which includes shareholders, employees and customers, the Chinese government is most often the major shareholder. There may be minority stakeholders as well. Some State Owned Enterprises now accept Western models of governance, which have a direct impact on how things are managed.

Though U.S. employees expect full disclosure and transparency, Chinese employees expect authority figures to make decisions in private and simply tell them what their role is in the overall plan. The common practice in Western countries to question authority goes counter to basic Chinese values of harmony and respect for hierarchy and authority.

New ideas typically come from the West both because of Chinese reluctance to question authority, and also because the Chinese educational system focuses on memorizing facts rather than critical thinking. On the other hand, because there are fewer rules in China than the U.S. it's possible to be more creative in China. Chinese people do have a sense of adventure and are often willing to give things a try, even though they may not come up with the new idea themselves.

In the U.S. there are many rules to prevent or limit undue influence, although lobbyists and other forms of influence through gifts are woven into our society, both above and under the table. In China you may pay someone to help you get a deal done. 'Red envelopes' (often a gift is enclosed in such an envelope), and what in the U.S. might be called bribes, are just part of the culture, and shared between people in trusted relationships.

With that in mind, we have to consider the best way to get a deal done. Here is some advice from a U.S. executive working in China:

> "First, I really try to understand the motivations and aims of the person I'm partnering with. In the U.S. you might simply ask them straight out what they want, soon after they first meet. In China it's better to hold back from the difficult questions on the first meeting. Have drinks and dinner a few times, then one time when it's only the two of you it could be time to begin a deeper conversation. You have to warm up to it. In China it's about relationships. It's important to understand how

and why the relationship is going to work before you get your message out there. You need to build the relationship before you talk about what you want. Then be smart about it. You're a foreigner and you don't know the system. There is no rulebook. It's more of a level playing field than in the U.S. In China you don't have court to fall back on if your contract doesn't work out. Your success is more tied to the trusted relationships you've built with your partners."

Historically, law was only a complement to Confucian ethics. Even today, Chinese still feel somewhat ashamed going to court, which is seen as not following ethics. Therefore the need to go the court to resolve the differences is not an optimal strategy in the Chinese environment.

In 2007 the fight between French food giant Danone and the Chinese soft drink giant Wahaha provides a good example for both the Chinese company to understand the Western business practice, and Western corporations to learn how to solve conflict with their Chinese counterpart.

The companies had been partners since 1996 in a business model *Forbes* magazine hailed as a "showcase" joint venture. And then it got into an extremely serious conflict. In the course of the bitter dispute Danone launched a series of legal battles against Wahaha and Wahaha's family owners. In the end it resulted in Danone's defeat. The Chinese media attributed the defeat to Emmanuel Faber, former head of Danone Asia Pacific, who took over the Asia operation in 2005. Mr. Faber, with a background on finance, merger and acquisition, was faulted for misjudging China's complex market and his lack of flexibility, which led to the conflict.

There is a clear and direct method to how the Chinese make decisions. To study it is to gain valuable insight into how to work within it. Americans seem to assume that as Chinese learn more about Western methods, they will of course adopt Western ways. Although Chinese are keen to learn Western methods, they sometimes sense a mismatch both in underlying cultural assumptions, and with what they see as slowness and inflexibility within otherwise efficient systems. It seems there is opportunity in bringing together the best of both systems.

Big trees catch the wind
that blows them down.

(IF YOU STAND OUT FROM THE CROWD, YOU
ATTRACT ATTENTION.)

树大招风。

© Can Stock Photo Inc. / joywang - Chinese's Dragon Year of the Ink Painting.

Developing Cultural Competence

A Chinese proverb states, "We will seek common ground while we accept their difference." Chinese tend toward acceptance of differences they find in other cultures. They see the U.S. as tending more toward evangelism, wanting to impose U.S. customs and values onto other countries. An example of a successful cross-cultural team might be equal numbers of U.S. and Chinese representatives running a company. This group would focus on seeking common ground together while accepting various opinions, and making decisions together.

U.S. culture accentuates the differences between individuals. There is an intention to make people feel special because they are valued for being different. Chinese feel very uncomfortable when they are singled out from the group, even for praise. They feel more comfortable when they are praised for being part of the team that helped the group succeed. Focusing on individual rights also slows things down in the process. Chinese prefer to focus on getting things done. Individuals know where their role fits into the process of the group getting things done.

China and the U.S. have very different orientations regarding strategies to get things done. It's important to remember that at a basic level we all have the same human needs, and we're all trying to accomplish the same goal. Keeping an open mind and being willing to see things from another culture's sometimes vastly different perspective may assist in building a bridge between different styles and strategies.

China is able to execute quickly because they often build consensus first, and mostly decisions are made by authority. The U.S. has developed management systems which can help Chinese companies be more effective. Despite a very complicated kind of system in the U.S. where diversity and dissent are valued and even idealized, by nurturing minority opinion they get new ideas. U.S. citizens are encouraged to think out of the box, and to try a new way of doing things just to see if it might work.

On the other hand, China has a clear hierarchical social order. The power of a Chinese society with a homogeneous majority Han ethnic group is that China has a population with similar values and aspirations. There is advantage with their cultural orientation toward valuing harmony and collective goals. Chinese seldom encounter diversity while they are growing up, even though China has 56 ethnic groups, of which Han accounts for over 90%. Children grow up with conforming values and similar ways of doing things.

In the U.S. to criticize someone publicly, challenge and debate their ideas, or confront someone doing something wrong ethically, is acceptable and perceived as being a good leader and a good citizen. In U.S. meetings, participation is expected even though the environment may not be safe. For Chinese to thrive in this U.S. environment it's necessary to change some of their behavior. Cultural intelligence and the willingness to change is a skill needed for global leaders. Chinese may feel very afraid to confront someone. They need to learn when it's needed, and to practice it as a new skill. Please refer to the chart –Guideline to Develop CQ.

Developing cultural competence starts with developing self-knowledge, which includes personality and the core value of a person. For example, for a Chinese person it's important to mentally change one's mindset and become more risk accepting of different styles and values, and have a positive attitude toward differences. Americans are relatively more open because they grow up in a diverse society, but China is a very conforming homogeneous society. Chinese need to acquire a cultural knowledge of U.S. society, including how to build trust within the U.S. culture.

Donny Huang, one of the authors, has developed an effective tool called WorldPass to measure cultural competence. The WorldPass model provides a structure to follow. Continued practice creates a virtual circle, and our core values are extended. For example, the Chinese have a core value of communicating indirectly, but when they work with people who have grown up in the U.S. they need to be direct. They are extending their base values. This develops a new principle that is acceptable to both Chinese and Westerners with whom they are communicating. In this way directness becomes part of the Chinese *global mindset*, so the core value becomes bigger, more extended, more global.

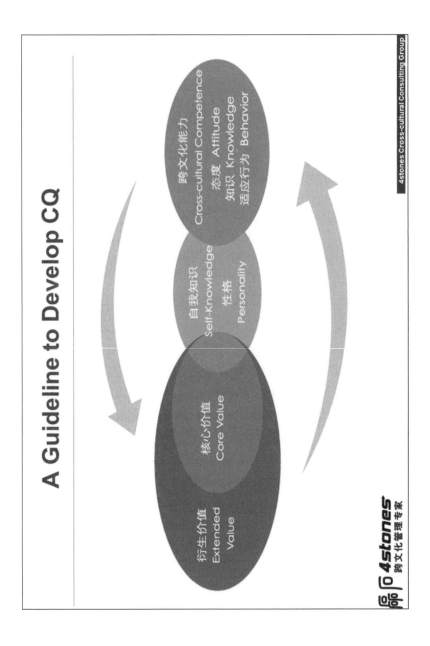

A Model to Develop Cross-Cultural Competence

China's unique business environment necessitates new innovative leadership development models that address the challenges of the Chinese context. The model described below draws upon many concepts, best practices, and research from the following sources: leadership (Dotlich, Cairo, & Rhinesmith, 2006), global leadership and cross-cultural management (Hofstede, 1981, 2001; House, Hanges, Javidan, Dorman, & Gupta, 2004; Hampden-Turner & Trompenaars, 1997), cultural intelligence (CQ) (Early & Angst, 2003) , international executive development (McCall & Hollenbeck, 2002; Rhinesmith, 1993; Lane & DiStefano, 1992; Gregerson, Morrison, & Black, 1998), intercultural communications (Ting-Toomey, 1999), China leadership development (Javidan & Lynton 2005; Lynton and Thøgersen, 2006).

Introduction to the Model

In the world of modern business, each day leaders in MNCs (multinational companies) must interact with colleagues, clients, partners, and suppliers across the globe, both face-to-face and virtually. This model focuses on helping leaders develop cross-cultural leadership skills that allow them to work and lead effectively in a multicultural environment. This model does not cover how to develop technical competence, but instead focuses on developing effective behaviors that drive results in a multicultural environment.

The model covers three types of competencies: *self-knowledge, cross-cultural competence,* and *extended values.* These three competences are interrelated and self-feeding to

121

You can't hide fire by
wrapping it with paper.

**(THE TRUTH WILL COME OUT.
NO WRONGDOING CAN BE
CONCEALED FOR LONG.)**

纸包不住火。

create a virtual circle. More in-depth self-knowledge will help development of cross-cultural competence, which will lead to development of more extended values. With more extended values, one will be more self-aware and able to demonstrate a high level of cross-cultural competence.

Self-Knowledge: As in all Western leadership development models, self-knowledge is an essential element of enhancing one's leadership abilities. Self-knowledge in this model includes understanding one's own personality and core values. By understanding personal core values, one will gain insight into his or her own cultural orientation. From an American perspective, when looking at China, due to the Chinese collective culture and its educational system, there seems to be significant focus on test scores and less emphasis on the actual ability to contribute value in the workplace. This, of course, is from the American viewpoint. In terms of cultural understanding, we need to realize that there are different interpretations from the different points of view, Chinese and American. There is not one universally correct way of doing things.

In terms of Western leadership development, Americans might say there is a narrow focus of curriculum design. Except in specialized majors, most college graduates do not have the opportunity to take courses in basic organizational behavior and psychology. Chinese graduates lacking this type of academic experience tend to have very limited self-knowledge, which in turn can create difficulties for leadership development as their careers progress.

As a result many graduates are unable to know what they want and are not well equipped to work in China's increasingly globalized market environment. McKinsey reports that only about 10% of Chinese college graduates are suitable for positions in foreign multinational companies (China's Looming Talent Shortage, 2005).

Personality here refers to the characteristic patterns of thoughts, feelings, and behaviors that make a person unique. In addition to this, personality arises from within the individual and remains fairly consistent throughout life. The *development goal* is to allow leaders to understand their personal traits and preferences.

Core values can be defined as those preferences, principles, and behaviors that are intrinsically embedded in oneself and that are an integral part of one's sense of self. When confronted with an unfamiliar set of core values, or when put in a situation where it is necessary to alter one's own core values, most people will feel somewhat uncomfortable.

The *development goal* is to educate leaders regarding the impact of culture on management and global business. It is also to push leaders to think about what their core values are and where these values come from. This will help them also plan hypothetical courses of action for situations where core values may come in conflict with national culture or corporate culture.

Extended Value refers to those preferences and behaviors in which you allow a range of flexibility that does not threaten your sense of self. The main goals of this model are to develop more extended values. In order for Chinese to work effectively in a multicultural environment, they need to develop extended values such as being more direct and transparent in their communication with international colleagues, clients and partners. They might also feel more comfortable giving and receiving constructive feedback, and being more punctual about time.

124

It is possible to find a personal comfort zone in the midst of sometimes overwhelming challenges. This comes from first of all knowing oneself, and being aware of one's own conditioned responses and cultural biases. Acknowledging to ourselves and preparing in advance for any specific personal needs we may have as we travel can reduce pressure, supporting a clear mind and a sense of personal wellbeing. This is always helpful when preparing to reach across a cultural divide with understanding and the creative energy it takes to really listen to the other person and keep an open mind.

Another key is being keenly aware of business and personal objectives before arriving, along with a strategy, and allowing the specific strategy to change as more wisdom is gained. Finding local people who can serve as mentors, having meals with key employees and developing trust with local leaders are also essential to success in the future.

This is part of how to build trust. As expatriates it's important to bring organizational culture to the country as well, balancing integration of the local culture and the company culture. Multinational values and methods usually overrule the local culture. Local employees can be trained in how to succeed in the company culture. At the same time foreign leaders learn the local ways of doing things, and teach local employees how to be an effective team within the company culture. Be clear about expectations. Let everyone know which behaviors are rewarded. Is the task or relationship more important? Are scheduled meetings contracts or is there consideration for urgent, important events of the moment that can override the schedule? How are ethics defined within the company?

What does a U.S. leader need to do to create an ideal situation so Chinese employees will, as quickly as possible, be functioning at a high level? This occurs best when the Chinese employee feels about their employer the same way they feel about their family. Because this doesn't happen automatically, it's necessary to create it intentionally.

Children in the U.S. grow up seeing diversity all around them, whereas Chinese grow up seeing similarity all around them. Diversity is inherent in joint ventures between people from different countries. Chinese people aren't necessarily afraid of strangers or people who are different, and they do have some interest in the differences. Reticence simply means that the society is not diverse, and not accustomed to different voices. Of course, this is changing as China changes.

The Chinese have a saying, "As long as you're good it doesn't matter. It doesn't matter whether the cat is black or white. As long as the cat can catch the mice it's a good cat." In this sense, diversity is simply not a factor. It's just about getting the job done.

What happens in China if you're a maverick and go your own way? As Donny says, "You get kicked out of the family, out of relationships. For example, if you work in a Chinese company, it doesn't matter how good you are if you are doing things differently. If you go against the family so to speak, the father/leader might kick you out. However, if you can prove yourself that you're really good, they may be willing to listen to you, even if you are a maverick."

The bird that sticks its head out is the first one who gets the bullet.

(STICKING YOUR HEAD OUT ATTRACTS POTENTIAL NEGATIVE ATTENTION.)

枪打出头鸟。

© Can Stock Photo Inc. / pauljune - Chinese landscape painting.

Merging Business Cultures

In the previous chapters we have explored various aspects of Chinese culture, discussed its generational gaps, and offered insight into the fundamental morals and characteristics of business practices. In this chapter we consider what each culture can learn from the other. We see many differences in the business cultures between Chinese and U.S. companies, and we are wise to take these differences into account. In particular, in this chapter, we will look at differences in such things as management and communication styles, decision-making, corporate and local cultures, among others. The most effective leaders and managers keep an open mind that some things will remain different and more appropriate when in another culture.

Lenovo gives us an excellent example of merging the two business cultures into one corporation. After acquiring the personal computer division of IBM, Lenovo went through a process of merging the Lenovo Chinese culture and the American IBM culture. The founder, Mr. Liu Chuanzhi, led the project himself to develop Lenovo's new corporate values and culture. This emerged as what has become known as the 5Ps. Lenovo's official website conveys this about their culture:

Our Culture

Our culture defines us … it's our DNA. We call it the Lenovo Way and it's the values we share and the business practices we deploy. It's how we address our day-to-day commitments. The Lenovo Way is embodied in the statement: We do what we say and we own what we do. That culture also drives how we work every day, utilizing what we call the 5 P's:

- We **PLAN** before we pledge.
- We **PERFORM** as we promise.
- We **PRIORITIZE** the company first.
- We **PRACTICE** improving every day.
- We **PIONEER** new ideas.

Our culture is what has enabled us to consistently raise the bar on delivering breakthrough innovations, award-winning designs and strong financial performance.

Co-author Donny suggests that when we look at the 5Ps, he sees the value **PRIORITIZE** company first is very Chinese, along with **PRACTICE** improvement every day. He believes this comes directly from the text of Confucian classics "Great Learning.' The Chinese text means making improvement every day is highly valued. Now, within Lenovo, no matter whether you are Chinese, Brazilian or American, you are expected to live up to the 5Ps. Lenovo was able to unite employees around the world to strive towards a unified organizational objective. Since then Lenovo revenues have grown in the past 18 consecutive quarters.

Gartner Research announced that in third quarter of 2013 Lenovo bypassed Hewlett-Packard, becoming the largest PC maker in the world. Lenovo is a wonderful example of merging the best values of both East and West, creating a competitive advantage in today's global business environment.

Management Styles

Historically in the West we worked under the assumption that the developed world must be superior, that the U.S. had the best systems and ways of doing business in the world. U.S. companies expected any country that wanted to develop their businesses would follow the U.S. blueprint. And China followed that lead. Thirty years ago China wanted to learn from super powers like the U.S. In fact, China still respects U.S. expertise and wants their citizens to learn as much as possible about U.S. business and governance. However, times have changed. China is finally now developing their own ways of engaging the marketplace, and their own unique brand of capitalism.

The Chinese have discovered a dilemma as they work with U.S. multinational companies. On the one hand the Chinese often value the systems that run the U.S. companies so efficiently. But on the other hand, they're baffled by the frustratingly slow process of getting upper management approval from their U.S. counterparts. The Chinese wait as U.S. businesses seem to drag their way through the so called "red tape" of bureaucracy while valuable time slips away. They wonder, "Why doesn't the CEO of the local U.S. entity have the authority to make important decisions?" While the Chinese want to implement the best of U.S. methodology, they don't want to copy or learn habits that inevitably slow down the growth and development of business.

131

A thousand friends are too few; just one enemy is too many.

朋友千个少，仇人一个多。

What could the West learn from China?   The manner in which the U.S. does business could improve if it took lessons from the Chinese way of life. In view of China's amazing feats of development over the past thirty years, there is much the West can gain from looking with an open mind at China's successes. China has radically improved their citizen's standard of living, and now has wide access to the outside world. Roads and infrastructure are superior, transportation connects mega-cities, buildings are well constructed, and Internet access is available on a dependable level. The truth is that something amazing is happening.

U.S. executives can learn something from the Chinese about adapting to rapid change, central control, respect for authority, building business on trust and working as a team. Some people in the U.S. find it politically sensitive to say good things about China, because they are uncomfortable with some aspects of the Chinese form of government. In addition, many Americans are increasingly aware of the percentage of financial dependency on China. Chinese people living through rapid social change in the past thirty years have developed the ability to adapt with an open mind toward the huge changes in order to survive.

When your cart arrives at the mountain, there is always a way for you to go through. When your boat gets closer to the opening of the bridge, it goes straightforward on its own.

(WHERE THERE'S A WILL, THERE'S A WAY.)

车到山前必有路，船到桥头自然直。

Career Path

Traditionally a U.S. citizen's career path is managed by the individual. The Chinese differ. Many times a Chinese organization would have more influence over an individual's career progression. In China today people work for the government, private organizations, and some work for State Owned Enterprises. The State Owned Enterprise is an important structure in China, because the government has retained strategic ownership of important parts of their society. It has limited free competition in more areas than we would in the West. In the West we have public utilities that are almost quasi-governmental, in that there is seldom competition for the electric grid of the power generating company. The Chinese concept is similar; simply more prevalent in China and in more areas within Chinese society. There has been a protection of certain industries and that has evolved into a lack of competition. Sometimes where Western technology is valuable, a joint venture is allowed with a Western company.

In the U.S. over the past several decades, some of the brightest and best of our graduates have been drawn into the lucrative fields of investment banking. The banking sector, although regulated, is the epitome of Western capitalism. The contrast in China would be that some of the brightest and best of their graduates would be attracted to working for the Chinese government, or State Owned Enterprises. It is not considered as attractive to work for Western multinational companies today as it was five to ten years ago in China. There is greater security, higher compensation, and greater status within Chinese society for persons choosing to work for the government or State Owned Enterprise. This is a major difference between the two societies.

Example of a State Owned Enterprise

Gary has had experience getting to know some of the people in a large Chinese State Owned Enterprise in recent years. In this example the State Owned Enterprise has two Human Resources departments: one that manages the leaders, and the second that manages all other employees. Regardless, both departments simultaneously report to the head of the State Owned Enterprise, allowing the top leader to retain control over all human resource decisions.

In this example Chinese organization, there are almost two million employees, six-hundred of which are leaders. The best and brightest graduates of the most acclaimed educational institutions want to be hired by State Owned Enterprises (SOE) because of job security, pay, and 'hidden benefits'. Once hired by the SOE, the individual may see their career path remaining within that organization for life. In the U.S. we do have some similarities with persons who choose to work for the U.S. or state government, or who see their life's career remaining with government work, or people who choose a career in the U.S. military. The HR department handles applications, evaluations, and chooses each employee's next assignment within the Chinese SOE. Like the U.S. military, employees don't choose where they go.

Employees can lobby, expand their networks and resources, and speak with their sponsors in an attempt to influence, but in the end they follow decisions sent down by HR. The HR departments track everyone's path and strategically place employees in specific jobs based on the overall plans of the SOE. The evaluation process is not transparent and the SOE operates as an extension of the Chinese government. The difference here is the matter of degree and how far this type of situation extends within the society, between what is taking

136

place in China or the U.S. In the U.S. we have considerable similarity for those people in the U.S. who work in various government jobs and in the military. One of the big differences is that in China not only do many people work for the government and military, there are also many State Owned Enterprises for which we have no equivalent in the U.S. in terms of government control.

In the end, many younger Chinese employees' goals are to get promoted and make money. A sense of personal achievement plays a smaller role. Because of the system there is less value put on a person's contribution to determine compensation. There is less evaluation of soft skills, soft metrics, company values, and growth value, which are often less valued. Chinese generally feel soft skills can be manipulated, and they don't believe soft skills can be effectively measured. They prefer to measure improvements in productivity. In China an individual's success depends on where they fit into the overall plans of the business. This ultimately affects the organization that pays the individual. Employees that behave in a way pleasing to their boss get promoted and are rewarded with advancement within the government. If an employee decides to go after a job in private business, they lose all earned credit with their SOE. This is similar to how it works in the U.S.

Motivational Differences: U.S. leaders sometimes report difficulties in managing Chinese employees. They often wish their Chinese employees would dream a little more, think differently, and have new ideas. It can be very hard for Chinese to think of how to do something differently. The U.S. encourages an entrepreneurial society. Steve Jobs, Bill Gates and other people who have been considered to be some of the greatest innovators in the world were often viewed as outsiders at first. Being an outsider in Chinese society has dire consequences. Chinese children are taught to fit in, in order to survive.

The son always takes after his father.

(LIKE FATHER, LIKE SON.)

有其父必有其子。

Work/Life Balance: The work/life balance in Chinese society is very different than in the U.S. A Chinese employee's parents often take care of their grandchildren, leaving the employee free to pursue their career. In China there seems to be less sexism, and more equal opportunity than in the West. A Chinese HR leader said that Chinese women listen first, are resilient and hardworking. They align with their goals, and often possess high IQ and EQ capability. They also can be tougher than U.S. women. The exception to equal opportunity seems to be sales jobs, which are often filled by men because the sales process in China often involves going out with the customer for ceremonial drinking. One young Chinese male professional reported a desire to learn U.S. sales techniques, wanting an alternative to the traditional Chinese sales process involving alcohol consumption.

Grooming Local Talent: When a Western multinational company opens a new entity in China, they often send seasoned Western leaders to train local leaders. Some say it takes about two years to prepare a senior Chinese new hire to be ready for their new responsibilities. During that time, Western expatriates may be hired with the expectation to help out for the first two years while the Chinese are being trained, and then move on. The expectation is to bring Chinese people into a position of management and authority. This means the Western leader has only a temporary position, so after about 18 months they often start to wonder where they will go next when their two year assignment is complete. They want to do a good job so they can go back to a better position. In order to groom locals successfully, the company should have a good talent development system to look after the expats. It is as important to focus on the expatriate's career path as well as focusing on the new Chinese leaders' career path. Preparing the expatriate before the assignment, and follow through support after the assignment is vital to good talent management and the successful outcome of their global assignment.

Trailing Spouse and Family: The number one factor that causes expatriate failure is not about the executive, but about their spouse. "Happy spouse, happy life", as one Chinese global leader commented. The executive is living within their accustomed multinational work culture, slightly different though it may be in location. The trailing spouse is living in the new country's environment alone for much of the time. There is probably a great deal of pressure on the executive to produce results and spend long hours at work. When the executive finally comes home they may just want to rest, and the spouse probably has been waiting all day for their company and attention. It's easy to see where conflict, because of different needs, might occur. In many situations the trailing spouse probably is not allowed to work, and may become bored. In China particularly there are difficulties for foreign spouses to get official work permits.

One of Gary's contacts was a U.S female executive posted to China. Her husband had previously had a professional career, and yet was not able to pursue that in China because he was prohibited legally from working. His only option was to become the supportive spouse, or house husband. This was a new role for him. His day was filled with taking care of the children, taking them to school and activities, taking care of the home, and volunteer work. Whether the trailing spouse is male or female, the same dynamic is possible. The spouse may have had a career that they're not currently able to pursue. They may become resentful, and may not feel totally fulfilled. They find themselves forced into a situation where there is only one option, which is to be the supporting spouse, not able to work outside the home.

140

In some extreme situations, they may begin to lose their own sense of self. They may become frustrated, bored and depressed, which of course detracts from being a happy, supportive spouse. This is an important dynamic that should not be minimized. It needs to be taken seriously, because the whole situation of moving a U.S. expatriate into a significant Chinese position could be undermined if this situation is not valued and addressed. The solutions are different depending on the individual couple. What we are saying from our own experience and observing others, is this situation needs not to be overlooked. Instead, it needs to be a primary focus so that the expatriate executive will be able to be successful, and the company will get value from having made the move.

There are a variety of solutions that usually are offered, but the circumstances and needs vary from family to family. They might include enlisting local resources to help with schools, work, shopping, and to help the family adapt and build a meaningful life in the new environment. Language and cultural training can also be very useful, and is sometimes provided by the company, or referred by the company to a trusted provider that's been used before. It's so important to have a strategy when you come to China. The main point we are making, is to take the situation of the trailing spouse and family seriously, so it is as positive an experience for the trailing spouse and family as it is for the expatriate.

There are no problems out there in the world, but foolish people create troubles in their minds.

(LEAVE WELL ENOUGH ALONE. DON'T CREATE PROBLEMS WHERE THERE AREN'T ANY.)

世上本无事，庸人自扰之。

Communication Style

In addition to developing a career path in a non-Western manner, the Chinese view the way in which they communicate in a different manner than the States. People who grew up in China have an inherent desire to make a positive impression at work, but often feel a bit lost in a Western team environment. Those who grew up in the U.S. exhibit behaviors Chinese would find offensive and embarrassing in their own cultures. These behaviors include openly expressing their opinions in public with assertiveness, confidence and enthusiasm, speaking out of turn, interrupting each other, and even speaking over each other.

In China communication has a very different tone and style. People take turns speaking, with the most senior member of the team speaking first, while others politely listen. After that person finishes speaking, others can respectfully contribute, being careful not to threaten the "face" of their superior. Chinese culture is very sensitive to the hierarchical order of things and treats elders and experienced leaders with an enormous amount of respect.

This amount of difference between communication styles can create significant gaps in team effectiveness. It can also lead to members from the Chinese culture to feel more isolated and frustrated in a situation where there are both Americans and Chinese. To address this, a leader might present cross-cultural issues from both the American culture and Chinese culture's point of view to increase awareness. The leader can help team members develop strategies to include input and meet everyone more closely at their comfort level. Giving behavioral examples of what works best in terms of the company's standards and cultural norms can also be very instructive for people from both cultures.

Decoding Chinese Decision-Making

To understand the Chinese decision-making process we need to understand what motivates the Chinese. Millions of Chinese people have left their original rural home towns, seeking a job in the new large cities in the east of China. Many times they have left their wives and children behind. Husband and wives may not see each other for months. This behavior could be extremely difficult for some people in some other countries to understand. The principle of family is important in China. In Chinese society, responsibility for family is one of most important motivators. Fulfilling their social role is extremely important for Chinese people.

A Western observer in a Chinese-led meeting may wonder how things get done when none of the participants is speaking up and contributing in the meeting. He's expecting a group discussion which will lead to consensus, which never seems to happen. Everything just seems to move along as though no collaboration is needed. When he finally asks a direct question asking for a decision, he may receive some form of polite 'yes', but when he looks back it's increasingly unclear to him what agreement was actually made. He walks away with two questions:

1. What actually happened in the meeting?
2. Where does he stand in terms of decisions made?

If he steps back and reflects a bit more, he may also begin wondering how the Chinese have been so successful in building entire mega-cities in a few short decades, when there is apparently so much time wasted in unproductive meetings.

144

What he's actually just witnessed is a meeting where decisions were announced in a harmonious way to the people involved in a particular project. What he doesn't see is what happens behind the scenes. Remember: Chinese people value harmony and authority. They prefer to think through their ideas in private until they are fully formed, and then offer their suggestions. Suggestions are offered in private to the person on their team with the authority to make the decision.

A good leader earns the respect of his employees by facilitating two way communication. He would schedule a private meeting with each person on the team individually to hear their ideas, and to pre-sell solutions he intends to present at the meeting. There may be any number of reasons for his decisions beyond what may seem obvious. There are many stakeholders for each project, and the leader's job is to find solutions that create harmony before moving ahead.

After meeting privately with each team member individually, the leader makes his decision and announces it during a group meeting. After the meeting, the leader goes back to each team member and asks each one if there are any issues they're aware of, and if they need any support to carry out their part of the project.

To a Westerner all of these meetings seem like a waste of time when one group meeting with one group discussion where everyone puts their cards on the table at the same time seems so much more efficient.

Chinese see wasted time in a meeting where someone is taking up the whole group's time, forcing everyone else to listen to their ill formed thoughts. They see this process as disrespectful, and want to say, "Come back when you have conclusions".

This carried over to our book interviews. Westerners were comfortable having a more abstract conversation, with ideas evolving throughout the discussion, and the Chinese were more comfortable with specific written questions presented in advance that they could answer during the interview.

Somehow the Chinese are far ahead in terms of execution of their plans, so Westerners may have something to learn from their methods. The result of the Chinese decision-making method is a cohesive team, with each member clear on their area of responsibility, and feeling wholehearted support for the greatest team effectiveness.

What can go wrong with this system? If the leader is more of a dictator than a facilitator, or leaves important team members out of the conversation, this can trigger a passive aggressive response. This could mean support is less than enthusiastic, and individuals may find indirect ways to undermine each other.

Don't judge people by how they look. Don't measure the ocean's volume by the bushel.

(A PERSON'S TRUE CHARACTER IS AS DIFFICULT TO FATHOM AS THE SEA.)

人不可貌相，海水不可斗量。

146

Profitability and Success

Similar to the U.S., Chinese businesses have some of the same motivations, such as to produce profit and succeed. However, the Chinese system is different from the West. Sometimes one part of the Chinese government or one part of society will be encouraged by the Chinese society to help another part of their business. This is particularly noted in State Owned Enterprises, where office space may be provided rent-free, or money loaned to the startup, because there is central planning by the government to determine which industries are important, and how to help those new enterprises.

The U.S. relationship between enterprise and government is much different. The U.S. is enterprise-oriented, and the government is there to facilitate growth and stability of private enterprise. In China the government is much more involved. In some ways of thinking about this, it's as if the government is the parent, facilitating the growth and health of the children, and involved with some more than others. State Owned Enterprises are perhaps the most directly linked to the Chinese government, but there is greater central state planning and development in Chinese society than the U.S. The government in the U.S. provides and facilitates, but usually does not control. In China the government has a much more prominent role.

Decisions made in the West by government or business can become unpopular, and citizens can use influence and popular opinion to change those decisions. In China, decisions are made by looking at the long-term view of what's best for the large 'family' of China, and ultimately China. Growth is a strong factor. If at some time in the future China's growth slows, there could be blame and political fallout. At this time it's not evident because China's exponential growth glosses over the inevitable challenges of fast growth.

Doing business in China has been described as walking in the dark. You can get to your goal, but you need faith to get there. In China the environment can change so fast, a key success factor is to continue adapting. Continuously thinking about how to align your organization's direction with what's good for China can help you navigate more successfully. China is essentially one extended family. When family members are in trouble, other family members help them out. Profitability is important, but it is also imperative to remember the importance of extended family.

The ancestors planted the trees, and their descendants enjoy the cool shade.

(WE ALL OWE A DEBT TO THOSE WHO CAME BEFORE US AND LEFT US SO MUCH.)

前人种树，后人乘凉。

Acquisition of Western Companies by the Chinese

In a recent five-year plan, the Chinese government included encouragement that Chinese companies begin to acquire more businesses outside of China. China is sitting an enormous amount of available cash, and it is possible for the government to dictate policy encouraging the use of some of this stockpiled cash to make acquisitions in the West. This would be a more active decision about using available funds, than simply the passive investments of the past, such as buying U.S. Treasury notes. Instead China will begin a large scale acquisition of potentially well-known global Western corporations. This whole concept may sound very strange to the West - a governmental five-year plan with significant encouragement that their companies use their private funds to acquire businesses internationally. Even more under direct control will be the State Owned Enterprises which are an extension of the Chinese government. They will have access to major amounts of funding for such acquisitions.

Of course U.S. citizens have always been free to acquire and create companies outside the U.S., but U.S. citizens would make these decisions based on their own private ambitions, which would not be tied to a focused government effort on the part of the U.S. This is a major difference. China is embarking on a centrally decided policy of significant acquisition of Western companies. This has very significant, far-reaching effects on the cultures of the two countries. How will it feel to Americans if twenty-five percent of the major brands that U.S. consumers use are known to be owned by the Chinese? Will Americans be prepared to work within the Chinese way of running a company? Will the Chinese understand how to work effectively with an American workforce? This is where *global mindset* will become vitally important.

Think about what it's going to be like when Chinese expatriates arrive in the U.S. to manage their new U.S. acquisitions. It would be natural to assume that the Chinese expatriates will be bringing their systems and preferred management styles. We have seen in this book that there are significantly differences in style between the U.S. and China. The Chinese will have the right, because they are the owners, to choose to implement Chinese ways of doing business within a company they own. Just as we have investigated conflicts occurring in China when there is a joint venture between American and Chinese, there will be conflicts occurring between Chinese management and American employees who report to the Chinese top management.

Most likely, at least in the initial stages, it's very possible they could send a number of Chinese senior expatriate managers to oversee the operations. These senior Chinese managers come, as we have discussed, with a different world view, communication practices and management systems. It will be important for the Chinese to develop their *global mindset* so that they are culturally sensitive. They will need to be able to minimize conflict and maximize synergy that occurs between the two cultures, as they develop their Western businesses that they now own.

Employee Engagement

Chinese view ownership and self-worth within a company in a completely different light than Americans. U.S. employees typically feel primary loyalty to their own careers, secondarily to their company, and third to their country. Chinese employees primarily feel loyalty to their country, secondarily to their company, and third to their own careers. Thus, if they have to decide between government practices or business growth, they may ultimately choose the top of the food chain, which is the government. Where employees feel loyalty, they feel more of a sense of ownership, and are more willing to go beyond what's expected to make sure things get accomplished properly.

As a global leader, you should position your business to complement government policies, rather than compromise them. But that doesn't mean the Chinese aren't dedicated to their careers. They are more willing to invest in the long term, developing products and strategies for future generations. Chinese workers often look around the office after closing time and find that their U.S. counterparts are long gone, while they remain working. They notice their U.S. co-workers taking personal vacation during critical periods for the company, which they wouldn't consider doing themselves. They know their company will need them even more during critical periods, and this takes priority over their personal vacation schedule.

A Chinese employee often puts less emphasis on their personal needs, and has more of a respect towards the overall needs of the group. They may want to take annual leave, but they'll think of how this affects both their teammates and their company. They'll realize they are needed and valued, so of course they won't take vacation during a busy time as it could negatively impact the overall goals of the company.

151

U.S. employees often think it's normal for people to value their individual needs and choices above that of the company.

Chinese employees bond with their company because of an expectation of longer-term employment and what's best for the organization. There is less emphasis on their individual agenda. Chinese think more in terms of extended family. It's not so much about me, and more about what's in the best interest of the larger family. Chinese employees are able to take a much longer view. U.S. employees often emphasize short-term goals, looking at this quarter's results for their stakeholders. Chinese are willing to invest and may not expect to have a return in a particular year, because culturally they have an emphasis on the long term. They may still need to show a profit on paper, but may be able to do so because another part of the government enterprise is providing needed startup support.

Chinese people wouldn't say the U.S. view of business is either right or wrong, but simply that it has implications towards the smooth running of the company. They point out this is another reason the Chinese company is more efficient in making progress toward their goals. The Chinese workforce traditionally is enormously dedicated to their company and views their job as a career, and one they intend to stay with hopefully for years to come. There are more people in alignment this way, working together towards the best interest of achieving the company goal. They all identify with the company's missions and act under the notion that their self-value and worth is directly tied to the company's success. Thus as a global leader, when you train a team and find the right fit, it is likely your Chinese based workforce will remain with you for the long haul. On the other hand, this is changing as the new generation understands the value of moving between companies to improve their salary and status.

152

Blending Western Multinational Headquarters with Local Chinese Operations

Regardless of their management experience, there is a learning curve when a Western expatriate arrives in China. There is a gap of knowledge, and it takes time to become acclimated. Managers will have to work diligently for years to understand the local culture in order to effectively implement initiatives coming from the company headquarters, which are expected to be implemented effectively in China. Managers should strive to understand the culture of their own company, and the company's culture of origin. They will need to become familiar with how to sensitively implement a Western directive within a Chinese context.

It turns out *global mindset* can actually seem an affront to some Western employees at headquarters without much global experience themselves. From the Chinese side, it may appear to the Chinese as an arrogant, U.S. ethno-centric environment. Especially when dealing with global cultures, it's essential to allow someone else to have a valid point of view. In a U.S. ethno-centric environment, there is an assumption that the Western traditions of law and management are superior. For instance Westerners may take for granted that contracts are enforced and courts can appeal. However, in China there is not the same consistency of law, which may even vary between different geographic regions of China. Contracts are actually more a memorandum of agreement at the time the contract is signed, and there is not a tradition of courts where the contracts can be appealed. Remediation is done through the trusted relationships the local leader was working to develop on behalf of their company's headquarters.

153

There is a different level of comfort with risk on the ground in China, than is seen when viewed from the Western headquarters, about the operations in China. Local risks are taken, but are taken in balance based on local customs and process. Local leaders feel great dismay when they hear from their Western headquarters, "You've gone native. You're just giving in to Chinese ways, choosing the path of least resistance," followed by a demand again to meet the U.S. headquarters-generated numbers. This may come from a lack of truly valuing the local Chinese context, and the need to manage and do business in a different way. There is no one right way to do things. If you want to be successful in China, it helps to actually think like the Chinese. If a company chooses to risk their assets opening a business in China, it's vital that everyone involved cultivate their *global mindset*. It helps to realize the Chinese have a highly sophisticated system that works very well within the Chinese culture. Real success and effectiveness will follow consideration and support of the local Chinese context.

Local Chinese leaders explain there is a difference in the starting premise between the two countries. The difference is not just language or culture, but that we see things from different perspectives. Western corporate headquarters are familiar with the idea of process, rules, regulations, and consistent ways of doing things. In China, things are done within the context of the organization, region, leadership, and specific situation. There is potential for a great deal of misunderstanding unless both sides take more consideration of the starting premise and operating practices on both sides.

154

Meaningful support from the U.S. parent headquarters, with an understanding of local culture, can make a huge difference in local staff's ability to carry out initiatives successfully. This can be realized by observing the following:

- Manage resources with more focus on doing tasks and less focus on reviewing tasks.
- Solve problems early and build better systems.
- Bring on enough project leaders, engineers and systems leaders to handle emergent situations in the field.
- Put the market first.

A company's headquarters should have a better understanding of the local culture even though they are at a distant location. Being aware of the local practices and ensuring your headquarters can appreciate local beliefs and customs will help to build a culturally conscious environment that can ultimately support long term success.

Generals and prime ministers were not born with dignity, but each man becomes himself through great effort.

将相本无种，男儿当自强。

Putting it All Together

With these considerations in mind, the cultural landscape may be getting easier to interpret. By reflecting on a company's profitability, success, ownership, decision-making and location, Americans may begin to understand Chinese standards and expectations in order to bridge the gap. Chinese often evaluate how they can trust foreigners based on whether the foreigners do what they say, whether they own what they do, and whether they deliver on their promises. Staying current with key Chinese contacts through email and personal time can help demonstrate a foreigner's dependability and trustworthiness.

Chinese leaders report they wish Americans would get to the point. Listening to continuous objections to every detail surrounding a process becomes very tedious and seems to waste time. They believe their meetings could be much shorter if discussion would simply focus on the task at hand. Their thought process is to figure out what you want, and then think of the ways to get it done. Then check in with the people who can do those things and have a focused conversation and inquire as to the outcome, status, and the kind of help each staff members needs from their team. China has an amazingly successful track record of getting things done. Their emphasis is on execution and the overall goal. How one gets to the goal is not as important and can vary. There is more emphasis on achievement of the objective. Arriving at the goal becomes the primary focus.

In the U.S. the way one gets to the goal is more important. It's the process. Chinese watch in amazement as U.S. initiatives never get to the goal, but become trapped in seemingly endless debate about how to do something. The Chinese would say, "Just start doing it. Stop thinking about how you're doing it." When they look at the American process, they see an advantage of their own political system. They observe so many things that don't get done in the U.S. because there's too much controversy and lack of alignment. Chinese people are more likely to accept the leader's goal without question, and there's more harmony and alignment towards achieving the goal.

Chinese notice how quickly U.S. employees are able to come into a meeting with little knowledge regarding the people with whom they're meeting. Yet they come directly to the point of the conversation. The Americans feel that's ok, and even feel successful when they seem to receive a positive response, or at least no resistance in the meeting. They may not be aware the Chinese are simply being silent to convey harmony in the public context. For the Chinese it's the relationship that's most important, and it's rude or improper to go directly to the purpose of the meeting so quickly.

Chinese believe actions always speak louder than words. They look to a foreigner's actions to prove their credibility. In their first meeting, they expect the foreigner to show respect and actually ask the Chinese to speak first. Ideally before the meeting the foreigner will have done some preliminary research. There should be no need for fact-finding after the meeting. Research would have already been done so there can be harmony and alignment during the meeting. At the first meeting, the foreigner would ask the Chinese to talk about themselves, their company and the situation. Trust and credibility are not built in one meeting.

Chinese initiatives get done through people. In China it's all about the leader. Leadership is about the leader's way of doing things. With Chinese hierarchy, the leader has almost complete control, so if the leader changes, the system also changes. Chinese employees respect the authority of the leader, and are willing to follow new instructions from the new leader. In the West there is more of a sharing of power. Process plays more of a role in U.S. In many multinationals the operating systems are the same in any country, so a leader can move from one country to another and the system stays the same.

Clearly, the Chinese culture and its people are becoming more and more familiar with the United States and the manner in which we operate. As our two cultures are introduced to one another and blended, they are both changing their expectations, reshaping their assumptions, and beginning to grow and change based on what is occurring around them. The Chinese carry extremely high expectations for those with whom they do business. They tend to not deviate from their fundamental beliefs. To bridge the gap, we have to focus on meeting each other in the middle, maintaining an open mind, and using our *global mindset*.

It doesn't matter whether a cat's color is black or white, as long as it can catch mice, it's a good cat.

(THE ENDS JUSTIFY THE MEANS. THIS QUOTE IS ATTRIBUTED TO DENG XIAOPING, THE LEADER OF CHINA IN THE 1980S, EXPLAINING WHY HE DECIDED TO ADOPT CAPITALISM IN A COMMUNIST COUNTRY.)

黑猫白猫，能逮着耗子的就是好猫。

© Can Stock Photo Inc. / konstantinks - Welcome to China, concept road sign.

Joint Ventures in China

The value of joint ventures lies in the ability for two businesses, organizations, or even individuals to work together to reach a common goal. For the purpose of this book, we are exploring the joint venture (JV) effort in China. This includes a mix of people from both a Chinese partner and a U.S. partner. Structures and internal processes differ greatly between partners in almost every way. Various negotiations are ongoing to find common ground and effective strategies. A key stakeholder on the Chinese side is often a State Owned Enterprise (SOE). This SOE is structured in a very traditional way. They may have an environment where there is a blend of the economic values of capitalism with the politically driven values imposed by the Chinese government. The SOE often has representatives from the government participating at many levels. In a sense these officials from the government who are employed within the SOE represent the interests of the people of China.

Learning is like rowing a boat against the flow. If you are not progressing, you are regressing.

逆水行舟，不进则退。

One of Gary's Chinese clients who is the CEO of a JV explains that the people who you originally negotiated with may not be the people you end up working with in a new JV. When you move from the deal stage to an operational stage with different players, you may have to reset your plans at the beginning of the business development phase. It is important for each partner to provide adequate human resources and counsel for the JV. A JV Human Resource toolkit could be presented to the JV CEOs from day one so they're familiar with procedures. A handbook can spell out compensation, benefits and incentives. In addition the handbook can define desired behaviors and catalog training available. Compliance is also a key JV issue and can be discussed in the handbook. The U.S. team will most likely want to spell everything out in detail before operations begin. The Chinese team will most likely want to set only overall intentions, preferring to define as needed, and within context, during the implementation phase.

One of the Chinese objectives is technological independence for China. U.S. companies need to think of about how much and what they can give up as Americans, and what they need to protect. This is especially true with State Owned Enterprises, as these are an extension of the Chinese government. The U.S. government has some sensitivity about transfer of certain technology to Chinese organizations. The United States is an old, stable country in terms of their way of life in the modern age, versus China as a very young country with wrenching social change, bringing them into a modern way of life. Though the foundations of Chinese society have been built for centuries, the degree of current change is enormous, and requires a different mindset and strategy to manage a successful business within this evolving context.

163

The key is to find harmony so the new JV can have a sustainable future. This means there needs to be an alignment of interest. There needs to be mutually acknowledged interest or gain. It's important to clarify what each entity wants. This needs to be good for China so you can find the right path, not just for the corporation, but for the country of China. This concept of thinking beyond the two corporations that are joined in the JV is the key for understanding a joint venture between the Western organization and the Chinese organization. Coming to China, the Western Corporation needs to realize that it's not just what is good for the two corporate interests, but that the Chinese will want to think beyond their own Chinese company to whatever this joint venture is going to bring in terms of value to China as a whole. They look beyond the interests of the two companies and what would be best for the joint venture.

Government and other entities will need to help in forming policy. In China control is from the government so it will be important to find a way that appears to bring value to the Chinese nation through the joint venture. For the U.S. and most Western countries it's solely about the interests of the two corporations, and the government is much less involved. One of the major differences in a joint venture in China is how central the needs of the nation are. This must be factored in when considering a JV in China.

A good year depends on how you plan in the spring. A good day depends on how you plan in the morning.

(DO NOT PROCRASTINATE, BUT USE YOUR TIME WISELY FROM THE BEGINNING.)

一年之计在于春，一日之计在于晨。

Differences Between Chinese JVs with U.S. Companies Compared with Companies from Other Countries

Since much of the audience for this book will be Americans attempting to transition into Chinese business ventures, it is vital to lay the groundwork for the impact U.S. companies have on Chinese business ventures, and the impact Chinese companies have on those in the U.S. In China, U.S. company JVs are treated differently from JVs from other countries. The difference occurs because of how well the other companies are culturally aligned. When China has a JV with a company from another Asian company, they have more cultural similarities. For instance, both cultures place an emphasis on relationships, as was discussed earlier. This makes it easier for both parties in the JV to understand each other, because they are nearer to each in their base culture. Asian companies have some cultural emphasis on the importance of relationships. China is looking to be a part of something that is changing, and yet there needs to be constant understanding and creating something new and value, and of benefit because of the blending of the two cultures. If the JV partner is not giving anything new then there is less value for the Chinese partner.

For instance, the French seem capable of thinking more broadly and being more flexible. The French seem to do very well as JV partners with the Chinese. One of the reasons for this is they do not let politics get in the way. The French also have state sponsored organizations that are similar to the State Owned Enterprises in China. Hence, the French system feels familiar to the Chinese. The French avoid politicizing the relationship, whereas the U.S. tends to let politics come into play. Sometimes this has a negative influence on the

166

relationship. China and the U.S. are very similar in that both believe themselves to be correct, and each trusts their own political environment. This politization is an important trend to watch, because it is inhibiting the development of some potential business between the two countries. We have seen some high profile cases reported in the media where politics has gotten in the way of doing business. This has occurred in the area of joint ventures in China, and certainly we are seeing it in the area of potential acquisition by Chinese of American corporations. This trend will probably become even more pronounced in the next few years.

When running a JV, culture impacts choices of what is emphasized. These emphases are different depending upon whether they come from China or the U.S. For instance, the U.S. company might have an emphasis on compliance and integrity and the laws that stand behind this. The U.S. company might prefer to emphasize safety over simply focusing on profit. In a U.S./Chinese joint venture there may be more control. Politics matter more because national politics between the U.S. and China impact the JV. There would be less involvement or concern about politics in a JV between another country and China because the other countries have less open conflict between national politics when compared with the U.S. and China.

Looking again at the relationship between the U.S. and Chinese partners, there will be differences in what is emphasized. It can be harder for the U.S. to be flexible. The U.S. is used to being in control. The U.S. is very open outside and conservative inside. The U.K., on the other hand, appears conservative on the outside and is actually more open on the inside. The French are more flexible. Europeans are used to dealing with different cultures and nationalities. The U.S.

has been more isolated and is not used to compromising when working with different nationalities.

A U.S. executive might go into a situation with the new JV partner and simply assume they'll get attention because they have been successful in the past, even though they have not yet established a relationship with those in the meeting. Apparent previous success and meritocracy form the basis of credibility in the U.S. In the U.S. one works hard, does well, and expects to walk into a meeting armed with respect for their past success. A U.S. entrepreneur expects their past performance will allow them to present a proposal, and they expect to be able to negotiate. In China or other Asian countries it does not work this way. Backgrounds are important, and the personal relationship developed is more important. There are many little ways to cultivate relationships in Asia. Effective strategies include bringing a gift, and/or asking others "How are you doing?" or "How is your family?", before commencing the business conversation. Americans do this to some small extent. In Asia it is considered very rude to go straight into business.

The king's daughter needs no worries about suitors.

(WHEN YOU'RE THE BEST AT WHAT YOU DO, PEOPLE WILL ALWAYS SEEK YOU OUT WITHOUT YOUR NEEDING TO GO IN SEARCH OF CLIENTS OR CUSTOMERS.)

皇帝的女儿不愁嫁。

Factors that Differentiate JVs in China from JVs in Other Countries

Management and understanding of Chinese government and politics is challenging for Western enterprise. Joint ventures in China differ from joint ventures in other countries. For instance, as noted above, in France there are State Owned Enterprises but there are fewer political demands than in China. State Owned Enterprise politics are very new concepts to U.S. entrepreneurs. To be successful, U.S. entrepreneurs must adapt to the politics involved in operating with an SOE. The traditional behaviors in the West are quite different from the traditional Chinese model.

As mentioned earlier, any joint venture or corporation operating in China needs to be aware that the needs of the nation will be taken into consideration, and that this will affect some decisions about how much support and in what ways the Chinese government allows you to do business. If you are a really small joint venture you may be able to operate without drawing much attention from government officials. This is also true if you are not in a strategic industry. However, if you are a larger or strategically important industry, you will have to make sure that your joint venture is aligned with and supports Chinese national interests.

Chinese Influence on the Joint Venture

As the manner in which we communicate grows and offers greater opportunities to build relationships across the world, we are consistently seeing an increase in the positive influence China is having on other parts of the world. As China

170

was growing quickly, it relied upon outside influences to shape its culture and business foundations. Now China is becoming a meaningful leader in its own right. When you're in a joint venture with a large Chinese State Owned Enterprise, there are several types of employees. There are totally new hires for the JV, and then there are people who have been allocated or seconded from each of the joint venture entities: U.S. and China. When you're in a joint venture with an SOE, the secondees from the China partner are watched and overseen by a director from the government working within the Chinese partner. These Chinese secondees are being paid well. The Chinese State Owned Enterprise really watches how the secondees act and perform. This oversight from their Chinese employer, the SEO, has great impact on business decisions. This may create may create disputes between goals from each of the JV partners.

To be fair, the U.S. partner also has secondees who have been allocated from the original American parent company. In a similar manner they are looking over the shoulders of their prior partner, and feel some loyalty to that U.S. company. So they also are not entirely free to be only employees of the JV. What we see is that although there are employees who have been allocated from both partners, they are sometimes caught in a situation where they have mixed loyalty. They feel some pressure to represent what they know as the separate agenda from their original employer. This is possibly at variance with the agreed upon or desired direction for the JV.

In China there is a nationwide mission. Rules change based on time and government needs. Things might change because of the two different countries' politics. Ventures between a Chinese and a U.S. company can be affected depending on Chinese – U.S. international relations as they go up and down in the global political arena.

If you accept food from someone, your tongue is softened; if you accept gifts from someone, your arms are shortened.

(ONCE YOU HAVE ACCEPTED BRIBES FROM SOMEONE, YOU DON'T DARE CRITICIZE THEM OR PUNISH THEM IF THEY DO ANYTHING WRONG.)

吃人家的嘴软，拿人家的手短。

There is a strong political backdrop if you are involved in the State Owned Enterprise. Language and communication styles are very different. The level of understanding is different. For instance, the goal is most important in China. The process is most important in the U.S. In China there is a long-term view and in the U.S. very often a short-term view. There are strong factors affecting many aspects of business.

Asian people and Chinese specifically look more holistically at the world than Americans tend to think. The Chinese see that the world is connected and interrelated. Americans tend to look less at the whole. Decisions are made in China by evaluating the immediate and long-term results. Chinese will say 'If it's good for the country it's good for the JV and good for the corporation'. In the U.S. if the corporation makes money, then the country benefits. Between the West and China, there is a difference in opinion observing these facts. From the Western point of view, the U.S. depends on individual corporations being allowed and encouraged to make money, and that makes America strong. The West is more corporate centered and China is more nationally centered. Western corporations need results now to survive. Chinese are concerned with making money over the longer term, but only if it serves the national interests.

The government in the West is better at simplifying and making rules so everyone can play the game well. In China they believe the world is more complicated. It is hard to lay out and agree on rules when looking at everyone's side. Chinese thought process does not work this way. Chinese are not usually focused on generalizing. They are better at making assessments. When they look at a specific case they can often provide a very good assessment judging that specific situation within a specific environment. Their way of thinking fits a fast-changing environment where there are constant reassessments

173

and change. From the Chinese standpoint Western logic works better in a situation where there are very few changes because rules can be adhered to and trusted over time. Chinese are good at coping with constant change because of their own recent history of the past 30 years. They have had incredible change transforming their society from a period of extreme communism to extreme state-sponsored capitalism. In the communism era, most Chinese were earning pretty much the same money, wearing the same clothes, living in the same housing. The options for clothing, living space, transportation, employment and education today in China rival and often surpass other countries. They have had to adapt and endure significant change in reaching the reality of China's success today.

Food and clothes won't take all your fortune away, but lack of planning will.

吃不穷，穿不穷，算计不到一世穷。

Suggestions for Joint Venture Success in China

With the ultimate goal of blending the differences in business cultures and folding them into one another to ensure a strong result, it is crucial to recognize the prevalent strategies to accomplish this goal. Generally, these fall directly on the following vital portions of any joint venture:

Chinese Management Style. According to the Chinese, when it comes to management, the goal should be to go out and discuss issues in advance of meetings and team situations so you do not have disputes at the meeting. The most important thing to realize is that even with the same goals there might be different management considerations. An effort must be made to begin to harmonize these differences. All of the parties involved should understand their specific responsibilities and emphasize communication as a team. To accomplish this task, upper management should focus on the following integral moving parts to ensure they are positioned for success:

- Acknowledge the need for hierarchy.
- Before you begin, bring people together to discuss their differences.
- Set up common agreed upon goals.
- Be realistic about what is most important.
- Put the best leaders available into the joint venture because they will be able to better bridge the differences.
- Emphasize training.
- Put effort into developing bonds between people.

175

Management style is often the outcome of culture: *who they are and how they grew up.* Effective leaders focus on getting to the root of each employees' belief system and motives, and treat each and every person as an individual.

Business Strategy. A second part of bringing joint ventures together is in creating a strong and direct business strategy. This includes leveraging available tools to help both sides understand the culture of both companies. To do this, leaders should observe the following key factors in the beginning when setting up the teams:

- Offer team members a cultural integration session.
- Adopt goals and objectives before the start of integration.
- Conduct a vision, mission and values workshop.
- Write down what is best about each team member.
- Create strategies and implementation in an ongoing way.
- Finalize rules in an all hands meeting.

Keep in mind that rewards and recognition of performance management are very important. Some ways to bring this out more in your organization:

- Have an all employees in a meeting to focus alignment.
- Emphasize goals and do not lose track of the goal.
- Think about what actions link with the strategy.

Expectations. Within any business venture, expectations are key when evaluating success and creating goals for each team member. Often Chinese leaders will want to break even within the first year. Be clear in business negotiations so the operating plan can satisfy mutual needs. The social side will be easier if you have regular meetings, and workshops about cross-cultural differences between East and West social practices. Think about having a cross-cultural coach for the senior executives. Consider the corporate cultures and how the two national cultures influence shared cultures. Then, fold these together with the following:

- Create a joint process.
- Respect each other.
- Communicate frequently and revisit goals.
- Be willing to revise and change as more understanding is developed.
- Have external vision.
- Understand the environment and what is required.

Chinese success is a measurement between oneself and ones peers. There is a very basic difference here with regard to expectations. In the West constant improvement is measured against improving one's own self, versus the Chinese perspective in comparison with peers. Chinese relationships are more harmonious when making certain that one is just a little bit better than their peers. Business goals can become a bridge between others' goals. Address how there is continuity of goals even when leaders are changed. Be willing to be flexible as circumstances change. Western values are aligned with what the corporation wants. Chinese values are aligning with what the leader wants.

Human Resources. More than ever, Human Resources plays an integral role in the development of their company's success. Simply put, they manage the needs of the team. Creating a strong and detail oriented Human Resources department is vital to keeping team members motivated. Human Resources should act as a support system, rather than an entity that implements punishment for violation of policy. To build a successful HR department:

- Be willing to spend time.
- Be flexible and giving.
- Provide more education.
- Avoid arguments.

The U.S. is a rules-based society. China is people based, so in this people based society the Chinese leader manages the people and to a lesser extent manages by rules. The West uses processes to manage people and rules. The West makes changes through changing the process. China makes changes through changing the person. An example is in the West a leader can be changed and yet the rules of the organization continue to guide everyone in a similar fashion as it was run under the old leader. When a leader in China changes, everything might change because there are no rules. What is important is the style and decisions that the individual leader is allowed to make.

The new CEO coming into a joint venture in China should have experience and knowledge in both cultures. They should have a holistic mindset. They should be focused on cultural equality in their thought process. The CEO needs to put the JV's interests first and have a mutual agenda that is balanced. Leadership at the JV should be inclusive. There must be considerable communication. Influence skills need to be used effectively. They should have good conflict management skills. Their personal attributes should include a high level of ethics and courage. They should be open and flexible, and have perseverance. They should have a local mentor. If they have experience as a CEO in China this will really help shorten the learning curve. They need to be open and they need to be willing to take risks.

Some U.S. joint venture partners have very strong company cultures. In considering a joint venture in China, U.S. companies need to really look at the motivation for the joint venture. *Is there really a desire or need for a joint venture?* If a strong culture exists in the U.S. company, a strong effort to get the majority share of the joint venture may follow. U.S. companies should focus on getting very qualified people who are able to deal with constant frustration and pressure. People should be put into the joint venture from the U.S. business who have detailed domain experience. Leaders must have credibility and be able to consider internal coaching. Leaders from the U.S. component of the joint venture should be aware of their past successes while accepting the fact that being a student again in the new culture is important to success.

Key issues must be prioritized and focused in the JV. Communication between partners is very important. Thoughts should be openly shared. Concentration should be on what is right for the joint venture. Partners must reach out and realize that they are not alone. Strong operating records must be maintained. Goals must be specific. Consistency must be maintained and goals must be realistic, and include progress reviews.

A unified team must be established to manage both parties' expectations well. JVs that are not doing well will require open minds and a really hard look. Everyone will need to look at each other as human beings. Success will depend on how well the true needs and wants of everyone involved is understood.

Being in a JV, especially as the CEO, is one of the best training experiences that can be given to someone for future success in meaningful roles within the corporation. Failure is a big risk that comes along with international ventures. It is a risk for the company and for the people involved. Individuals will gain because of the experience. In the West the company potentially loses the person if they fail, or even if they are successful. The Western company needs to consider how to focus on maximizing return on investment. If there is success the person will have learned to adapt. They will bring international business experience back to the Western corporation. In the West too often the corporation that sent the person to the JV fails to realize the value gained and capitalize upon it. Their international experience is actually minimized in some cases. Corporations involved in international business need to focus on the large investment made and how to get a return. Leaders must have insight into how individuals sent overseas to work in a JV have had to work in the field in a very different and difficult situation. They have gained skills that are immensely valuable in a world increasingly dependent on having a *global mindset*.

If you don't want people to know what you did, you'd better not do it.

若要人不知，除非己莫为。

© Can Stock Photo Inc. / sannare - Forbidden city in Beijing, China.

Global Mindset Applied

Our world is changing rapidly. Just as emotional intelligence has become popular during the past decade, we believe that *global mindset* is going to become one the most important new skills of this decade. Bridging the gap between different cultures and regions of the world will be the difference between those companies that become global powerhouses and those that fail at the international level. Getting along effectively with people within our own culture can be challenging enough. Imagine the great challenge you may have when relating to a country with a completely unique set of business norms and socially accepted standards. As the world becomes flatter and we are all more affected by our neighbors, we add a multicultural overlay to the mix. This creates exponential nuances, each of which affect accurate interpersonal communication, assumptions and interpretation of any business message. In order to work and live effectively in the new global environment, we all need to become more aware of our own cultural biases and filters, and those of the people we work with.

More people, more strength the power is; more firewood, higher the fire is.

(THERE IS STRENGTH IN NUMBERS.)

人多力量大，柴多火焰高。

We are experienced coaches who specialize in *global mindset* and cross-cultural coaching and training. We help our clients become more successful in an international setting by overcoming their fears and learning to navigate the differences between cultures. We help them become more culturally sensitive. Aspects of *global mindset* have been called cultural intelligence, cultural quotient or CQ. This has been described as a measure of an individual's ability to engage successfully in any international environment or social setting. For our purposes we're focusing on CQ in business. Our behavior is deeply influenced by our own cultural background and upbringing. An awareness of and appreciation for how others think, act and are motivated in other cultures is essential to achieving our desired business outcomes.

Global mindset is developed and conveyed through our cognitive, physical and motivational experiences. We first develop a greater awareness of our own and other cultures. We notice similarities and differences. We may begin to realize there are even differences in how we move our bodies to convey various messages. We find that a common unconscious body movement or facial expression in our culture may convey a very different and potentially unwanted message to the other culture. It's important to notice and interpret subtle body language in another culture, especially when we're not getting the verbal response we're expecting.

Finally we begin to realize that even the means of gaining rewards, forms of acceptance and support, and definitions of success can vary widely between cultures. For expatriates entering foreign environments, not knowing what to expect and perhaps feeling overwhelmed and disoriented as they encounter multifaceted differences, culture shock can be a very real experience.

When you are drinking water, don't forget those who dug the well.

(DON'T TAKE FOR GRANTED THE HARD WORK OF THOSE WHO CAME BEFORE YOU.)

喝水不忘掘井人。

Seeing Ourselves Through a Global Mindset Filter

While it's easier to see others somewhat objectively, it's sometimes more difficult to see ourselves clearly through the lens of another's point of reference. As we reflected upon the similarities and differences between Chinese and U.S. cultures, and what works well and doesn't work so well in each society, we have come upon an interesting insight into ourselves. We have discovered that both cultures see themselves differently than they appear. Each country's self concept is not their actual reality, especially as seen from the outside. That said, we note that we are somewhat limited in our ability to see each other clearly, because we come with preconceived notions about ourselves and each other.

The U.S. has historically seen itself as a flexible, open society which promises its citizens freedom. They see the Chinese as historically having a closed society which greatly limits individual freedom. The Chinese has historically seen itself in terms of its deep traditions over centuries, as a very static and stable society. Some Chinese have told us that they view the U.S. as perhaps a young nation with the more (adolescent values) of short term gratification, and with an unfocused affect due to the influence of the masses upon public policy.

If one steps back from these conditioned perspectives, it's interesting to see the unexpected mirror image within each society. What we actually are can appear almost the opposite of how we see ourselves. For instance, although Americans think of themselves as individualistic and flexible, in truth there are many rules and structures that can sometimes impose limitations on our response to new challenges. Although we think of ourselves as flexible, when compared with the Chinese approach to flexible laws, we are not as flexible and open as we think.

China thinks of themselves as more static and traditional. But actually their system, without set rules and contracts but rather memorandums of understanding, allows them to adapt more quickly. A business in the U.S. that wants to change a contract has greater difficulty.

In the U.S. when there is a new leader, the rules and contracts remain the same, providing consistency. In China when there is a new leader, the whole structure can change according to the way the new leader chooses to lead. From that perspective China is a very flexible, individualistic society, whereas the U.S. is bound by rules and traditions which are not as flexible, and yet provide consistency.

Why in U.S. society do we devalue leaders for 'flip flopping'? Does this mean if a leader learns something new, or if conditions change, that they can't change their mind? How can a person or country move forward effectively in today's world with its constant new changes? This attitude seems to support the 'don't confuse me with the facts, I've made up my mind' perspective.

The Chinese would look at this and wonder why we limit ourselves this way. Is our structure so important? This stance can lead to less success in the world because our world is becoming less predictable, not more. We may be judging both ourselves and each other incorrectly. We are somewhat different from our perception. Our self concept is at variance with our reality.

Global mindset can help us to acknowledge that the Chinese have been able to navigate fast growth in a short amount of time within their context. Their citizens have grown accustomed to great change and have developed systems to keep their society intact while dramatically expanding their infrastructure and lifestyle opportunities.

While the Chinese have encouraged Western influence in business and technology so they could learn from us, we might benefit by learning from them in some of the ways they have been able to excel.

Suspicious minds create ghosts in the dark.

(A PERSON ALWAYS LOOKING FOR PROBLEMS SEES THEM EVEN WHEN THERE IS NOTHING.)

疑心生暗鬼。

Conclusion

We believe the development of *global mindset* is a requisite for success in business going forward. This will require increased self understanding, openness and tolerance regarding others' ways of life and management. Only by being truly open to new ideas and new ways of relating to one another can we capture the opportunities available in our new, fast-changing world. This does not mean that we have to give up our own beliefs and values. Instead, by exercising our increased understanding, openness and tolerance we are able to build trust with people who are different from us. This gives us a competitive advantage.

We wrote this book with a pragmatic purpose in mind. We hope we have taken you beyond simply valuing the other culture, to actually incorporating what you have learned into your business strategy. Our hope is to guide you to a new, more advantageous position as you become more proactive in the development of your own *global mindset*. Looking through the lens of your own *global mindset* will help you navigate more successfully so you can take greater advantage of business opportunities with China and the U.S.

A thousand-mile journey starts at the place under your feet.

(THE LONGEST JOURNEY BEGINS WITH A SINGLE STEP.)

千里之行始于足下。-Lao Zi

© Can Stock Photo Inc. / Elwynn - Chinese painting of bird, traditional ink artwork.

Assessment Tools

Looking through a ***global mindset*** lens at the intersection of Chinese and Western environments and practices can be very enlightening. We hope you are beginning to feel better equipped to work within China. To explore a more detailed and instructive prism through which to view this new global setting, a deeper dive into one's own conditioned thinking can illuminate where some of the cultural gaps in understanding may be for you personally. As an American, the ability to truly immerse ones mind into how the Chinese communicate with one another and view their identities and place in society is valuable. This can be complicated by U.S.-centric beliefs of which we are often consciously unaware.

Simply keeping ones antennas tuned to social interactions can be another helpful tool. Suppose you are having a conversation with a potential business partner who happens to have grown up in another culture. You suddenly sense things have just gone off track. You have no idea why, or how to bring things back to a place of equilibrium and trust. You simply are not equipped with the background and training to understand the other side's vantage point. Without some context for the basic ways cultures can differ from one another, as well as how people from other cultures interpret certain words, gestures, tones, and concepts, creating a bridge of trust and productivity can be enormously challenging. To accomplish this end, let's take the time to visit with some of the experts in the area of globally minded management.

To more fully comprehend the intricate concepts supporting China's unique and distinct business practices as different from the West, following are some tools which may help you test your current ability to see things from another perspective. Using the resulting data as a guide towards how one can improve rather than as a static indictment of deficiency, can prove very helpful in developing ones own proficiency in *global mindset*.

This book is written based on the authors' actual coaching and training practices. The authors use several tools in their *global mindset* work. The following sections contain a synopsis of the topics and questions covered in three of those assessment tools.

Distant water cannot quench urgent thirst.

(THE PROMISE OF SOMETHING TO COME IS OF NO HELP WHEN THE NEED IS IMMEDIATE.)

远水解不了近渴。

Global Mindset Inventory
http://globalmindset.thunderbird.edu+

We authors are all certified in using Thunderbird's Global Mindset Inventory. We find it a very useful tool in helping global leaders improve their awareness of the various aspects of *global mindset.*

According to Mansour Javidan, Ph.D., Mary Teagarden, Ph.D., and David Bowen, Ph.D. of the Thunderbird School of Global Management, companies often send executives overseas on the assumption that a successful domestic track record is a good predictor of success in the global arena. "Unfortunately, such assumptions often lead to painful experiences. Conventional wisdom surrounding effective global leadership development is missing a key ingredient. We believe this key is Global Mindset, a set of individual attributes that help a global leader influence those who are different from them."

*Their concept of **Global Mindset** consists of three dimensions:*

1) **Intellectual Capital**—global business savvy, cosmopolitan outlook, and cognitive complexity.

2) **Psychological Capital**—passion for diversity, quest for adventure, and self-assurance.

3) **Social Capital**—intercultural empathy, interpersonal impact, and diplomacy.

195

If a multinational company wants to operate in China effectively, it is essential to make training and development an important part of the organization. Ideally employees could familiarize themselves with specific regions of the country. All employees should be involved in detailed and global training in order to understand other cultures and how they relate to them both personally and professionally. This can often be accomplished through being more conscious of one's own culturally based conditioning. Once consciousness is developed, it can lead to being more aware of how the use of words, gestures, tones and strategies may help to create solid work relationships with others.

Learning without thinking is being ignorant (because nothing is gained). Thinking without learning is dangerous (because one can get confused).

学而不思则罔，思而不学则殆。

Relationship Strategy Tool
www.GaryRanker.com

In Gary's CEO coaching practice, he uses specific tools with his ***global mindset*** coaching to help develop leaders from various cultures. This has worked very effectively with his Chinese senior management clients. With a distinct focus on transitioning successful CEO's to a more globally minded leadership structure, Gary's work is hyper-focused on developing the skills and tools which help to turn local leaders into global ones. To do so, Gary implements a valuable cultural assessment device that aids leaders in understanding their aptitude and fluency in global development.

The Relationship Strategy Tool brings interpersonal relationship issues into a practical realm where they can be dealt with more easily. It helps a person prioritize the people who are most important, identify what they want to achieve and prioritize what actions they can take that will help the relationship to work more in their favor so they achieve what they want. It systemizes interpersonal actions. Far from being manipulative, it allows for conscious choice and focused effort, resulting in much greater productivity with much less effort and human angst.

A brief overview of the process:

1.   Identify the five key people in your work life. When you look at the relationship, consider these questions:

- How you feel when you have interaction with that person?
- Look for patterns. Is there something you can learn from what you notice?
- This exercise helps a person to begin to understand themselves as well as the key people around them.

2.   Think of your major goals.

- How supportive are each of these five key people?
- Are they passively or actively resistant or supportive?

3.   Next is to identify your highest priority needs from each person. What do you need from each of them in order to achieve your goals effectively?

4.   Create an action plan and follow up.

WorldPass CQ Assessment
www.4stones.net

You're having a conversation with your counterpart who happens to have grown up in another culture, and suddenly you sense things have just gone off track. You have no idea why, or how to bring things back to equilibrium and trust. Without some understanding of the basic ways cultures can be different, and how people from other cultures interpret certain words, gestures, tones, and concepts, creating a bridge of trust and productivity can be challenging.

If a multinational company wants to operate in China effectively, it's essential to make training and development an important part of the organization. All employees should be involved in the training in order to understand other cultures and themselves, to become more conscious of their own culturally-based conditioning, and to become more aware of how they use words, gestures, tones and strategies that may or may not be helping them create solid work relationships with others.

The following is a highly simplified listing of dimensions from the Worldpass CQ Assessment developed by co-author Donny Huang.

Person to Person

Equality / Status, Hierarchy
A/ Equality: You believe people should all have equal rights and an equal voice.

B/ Status, Hierarchy: You believe decisions should be made only by people in positions of authority, and your job is to obey and support their decisions.

Individual / Group Identity
A/ Individual: You think in order to build a strong group, it's important for each individual to voice their opinion.

B/ Group: Though you may have your own ideas, you support the viewpoint of the group because group harmony is more important than individual opinion.

Direct / Indirect Communication
A/ Direct: When you have something to say, you simply say it, and you would like to hear a clear, honest message from the person you're speaking with.

B/ Indirect: Politeness is of utmost importance to you. You're able to decode subtle cues in another's communication to understand their message. You're uncomfortable with direct questions from a stranger.

Equal / Contextual Treatment

A/ Equal: You trust the written agreement which has been signed by reliable parties, more than a handshake and verbal permissions.

B/ Contextual: You prefer to solve problems and achieve goals through trusted relationships and the reliability of their connections, rather than relying on legal contracts.

Person to Business

Task / Guanxi Focus

A/ Task: Tasks are building blocks to achieving a goal and any human interference in completing a task should be minimized as much as possible.

B/Guanxi: While you understand the value of completing a task, you believe maintaining a good relationship is of higher priority than the immediate task.

Fact / Intuition Decision-making

A/ Fact: You like to focus on the facts, and draw a conclusion from empirical evidence.

B/ Intuition: You synthesize facts and other relevant factors, but weight your final decision on what feels like the right thing to do.

Internal / External Locus of Control

A/ Internal: You make your own decisions.

B/ External: You trust the group or your superiors to make the most appropriate choices for you.

Person to Time

Inflexible / Flexible Scheduling

A/ Inflexible: You plan in advance, get agreements, and expect others to show up at the appointed time as agreed upon.

B/ Flexible: You make schedules, but how you actually spend your time depends more upon the needs that come up as the day unfolds.

To move a tree might kill it. To move people may bring them new life.

(MOVING TO ANOTHER PLACE TO LIVE AND WORK MAY GIVE YOU A CHANCE TO START A NEW LIFE.)

树挪死，人挪活。

References

In addition to many interviews with executives working in China, the following articles provided additional background for this book.

Beechler, Schon and Javidan, Mansour. 2007. Leading with a Global Mindset. *Elsevier* Ltd.

Jin, Guantao and Liu, Qingfeng. 1992. *The Cycle of Growth and Decline – On the Ultra stable Structure of Chinese Society (in Chinese)*. *The Chinese University of Hong Kong*

Cohen, Warren I. America's Response to China: a History of Sino-American Relations (5th Ed). *Columbia University Press, New York.*

Kennedy, Paul, *The Rise and Fall of Great Powers*, New York: Vintage Books, 1987

Huang, Donny. 2010. Leadership in China: Challenges and Practice. *2010 Pfeiffer Annual: Leadership Development*, edited by David Dotlich, Peter Cairo, Stephen Rhinesmith and Ron Meeks.

Huang, Donny. February 2006. Mentality, Mindset, Mianzi: How to Avoid a Crisis. *Business Forum China.*

Javidan, Mansour, Ph.D., Hough, Ph.D., Leaetta, Bullough, Ph.D., Amanda. Conceptualizing and Measuring Global Mindset: Development of the Global Mindset Inventory. Thunderbird School of Global Management.

204

Ranker, Gary, Phipps, Mike and Gautrey, Colin. 2008. *Political Dilemmas at Work: How to Maintain Your Integrity and Further Your Career.* Wiley.

Website: http://en.wikipedia.org

Website: http://www.theworldofchinese.com

Website: http://usa.chinadaily.com.cn/epaper/2013-05/31/content_16552293.htm

Website: http://www.lenovo.com/lenovo/us/en/our_culture.html

Macguire, Eoghan., Anderson, Becky, *'Silk Road' railways link Europe and Asia".* CNN, June 27, 2013

"Global mindset is the ability to step outside one's base culture, and to understand there is no universally correct way to do things."

— Dr. Gary Ranker

Dr. Gary Ranker

Global CEO Coach
Gary@GaryRanker.com
www.GaryRanker.com

Dr. Gary Ranker is one of the fathers of the coaching profession, having been approached by GE in 1989 to be one of Jack Welch's first coaches to help top managers change behaviors and become even better leaders. He is cited by Forbes as being one of the top five executive coaches. London's Financial Times describes him as one of 50 most important thought leaders.

Gary has worked and lived on four continents, and has been a CEO in various international locations for Hallmark Cards and Textron. He brings a truly *global mindset* to his international practice coaching CEOs and very senior executives of Fortune 500 companies around the world. He spends 90 percent of his time away from his home base in New York City, traveling over 500,000 miles per year visiting his clients. In recent years he has spent over 300 days in China.

"Global mindset leadership is the ability to understand ourselves — not only our personalities but also our core cultural values — and to lead and manage effectively across cultures."

— Donny Huang

Donny Huang

Cross-Cultural Consultant
donny_huang@4stones.net
www.4stones.net

Based in Beijing, Donny is Founder and Managing Director of 4stones Cross-Cultural Consulting Group. He helps both international and Chinese national executives and leaders develop cross-cultural competence, including Lenovo, Huawei Technology, ZTE Corporation, Motorola, the World Bank, UBS, Royal Bank of Scotland, Areva, Agilent, and Telkom Indonesia. He is regarded as the top cross-cultural management specialist in China by Chinese media.

Donny Huang has published over 30 articles in the Chinese business press, and contributed to *Managing Cultural Difference* (Sixth Edition) by Dr. Robert Moran. He holds an MBA in International Management from Thunderbird School of Global Management, U.S., studied Cultures and Leadership at Hawaii's East-West Center, and Intercultural Communication Institute in Portland, Oregon, U.S.

"Our cultural environment is so multifaceted it's hard to imagine anyone responding with finesse to every cultural equation. It takes patience with oneself as well as others to navigate successfully."

— Marilyn McLeod

Marilyn McLeod

Coach, Author, Producer
Marilyn@CoachMarilyn.com
www.CoachMarilyn.com

Marilyn McLeod is the author of 12 books (one #10 on Amazon), and executive producer of her television show *Consider the Possibilities*. She has worked with Marshall Goldsmith and Gary Ranker for over 10 years. She managed a successful coaching project with Marshall, and presented with him to senior leaders in the Air Force, and to the Haas School of Business, University of California.

As Founding Director of the Thought Leader Partnership of the Marshall Goldsmith School of Management, Alliant International University, she brought together students and world-class business leaders for dialog and mentoring. Marshall and Marilyn published articles together, including "Peer Coaching Overview" and "Thought Leadership: It comes from outside and inside", published by *Leadership Excellence*. Most recently she developed a Thinkers50 mobile application in conjunction with Thinkers50. She became certified in Thunderbird's Global Mindset Inventory in 2011.

**When you come to another place,
follow its customs.**

(WHEN IN ROME, DO AS THE ROMANS DO.)

入乡随俗。

Thank you for reading our book. If you enjoyed it, won't you please take a moment to leave us a review at your favorite retailer?

Dr. Gary Ranker, Donny Huang and Marilyn McLeod